Self-Care
for
New Moms

Self-Care

for

New Moms

Thriving
Through Your
Postpartum Year

Corinne Crossley,
licensed medical health counselor

Skyhorse Publishing

Skyhorse Publishing books may be purchased in bulk at special discounts for sales promotion, corporate gifts, fund-raising, or educational purposes. Special editions can also be created to specifications. For details, contact the Special Sales Department, Skyhorse Publishing, 307 West 36th Street, 11th Floor, New York, NY 10018 or info@skyhorsepublishing.com.

Skyhorse® and Skyhorse Publishing® are registered trademarks of Skyhorse Publishing, Inc.®, a Delaware corporation.

Visit our website at www.skyhorsepublishing.com.

10 9 8 7 6 5 4 3

Library of Congress Cataloging-in-Publication Data is available on file.

Cover design by Daniel Brount
Cover illustrations by gettyimages

Print ISBN: 978-1-5107-5515-4
Ebook ISBN: 978-1-5107-5516-1

Printed in the United States of America

*For the loves of my life—Croz, Bear & my lucky bug. I love you all the time.
For all the moms, but most of all my mom. Proof that a good enough mother is
perfect for her children.*

Table of Contents

Introduction

I am twenty years old and more than twelve years away from becoming a mother. I sit low on the leather couch despising the overhead fluorescent lights. My new therapist Heidi sits opposite me, her face gentle and welcoming. I feel like a mess. Hard-charging through the last three years of my academic career, when professors started urging me to consider graduate school, I splintered. I feel full-on adulthood rushing at me like a bullet train. I can't eat. Sleep is spotty. Tears are constant. Occasionally, I wretch from anxiety.

Heidi meets my eyes and emphasizes, "There are three things that we all need to do every day." She ticks off each with a finger, "You have to eat. Even if you don't feel like it. At least a little. You have to regulate yourself with a steady amount of food. Second, sleep. Six to eight hours. I know it's hard, but you need sleep. Third, you have to interact with people. Preferably, out in the world. These are the things you need to do. They aren't cure-alls. But, when we don't do them, things get a lot worse."

I nod solemnly. Always eager to please others, I have my marching orders. Eat, sleep, talk to someone. Got it. Except food makes me feel sick, I can't stop my brain from reeling, and I can barely hold my shit together on the train ride to campus. But okay. I'll try anything at this point.

It takes several months, but in a game of inches I pull away from anxiety's vice grip. I keep eating and eventually remember when I am hungry. I try sleeping and then someday it lasts through the night. I go to class and then work my way back to social gatherings, then stores and malls. The sobbing stops. The shaking stops. Hand over hand, I gain more rope on my side of the tug-of-war with my brain. With good therapy, support, and the wish to do other things, I got better. I graduated, got a job, hung out with friends, met a really good guy, went to graduate school for counseling (keeping good on my vow to help other people struggling with mental health issues), built a therapy practice, and had a couple of babies. Bullet points, but you get the idea.

That day in my therapist's office is now literally half my life ago. Since then, in the hundreds of hours spent in school and trainings, I never heard anything more vital than the words that Heidi offered me that day. Eat, sleep, be in the world. It was our work together where the importance of self-care became evident. Now that I am a therapist, just about every single client who comes to me in crisis gets what I call "my Heidi speech." We all need a foundation of self-care.

Self-Care for New Moms?

What do we mean when we say self-care? "The term self-care is so oversaturated that people misunderstand the definition of it," Emily Silver, NP, responds when I ask about her definition of self-care. Co-owner of Boston NAPS, an infant care and parent education company, the issue is close to her heart. "As moms, our first mistake is we confuse self-care with basic human needs like eating or showering. I want people to do those things, but that's not enough." Passionate about the health of babies and moms, Emily explained how she and her co-owner Jamie O'Day used essential tenets of self-care to inform the name of their practice. NAPS is an acronym intended as a reminder for self-care.

N is for nutrition or nourishment. Prioritizing feeding yourself sustaining meals and snacks is a major cornerstone of self-care. This is especially the case for new moms. We spend forty-five minutes straight packing diaper bags with bottles, nursing covers, diapers, sippy cups, and teething puffs, but forget to include a sandwich for ourselves. Adequate nourishment is a non-negotiable feature of self-care.

A is for alone time. Yes, time for yourself is an essential. Going for a baby-free walk, reading a book, or watching a show that does not involve puppets or cartoons.

P is for people. Not only does this entail being with people in general, it is important to find your support system. Who are the folks who have your back? What new connections can you make?

S is for sleep. Sleep is essential to your mental and physical health, and a rare commodity in the life of a postpartum mom.

Twenty years after that initial therapy session, though Emily is in an entirely different profession, she reiterated the same tenets I heard there.

Self-care is not a luxury. It is a necessity. Motherhood is a marathon, yet we treat ourselves as anything but athletes. We often feed our babies, partners, older children, friends, and even pets before we sit down to a meal for ourselves. Imagine asking a marathoner to run her race fueled on leftover chicken nuggets and three hours of sleep. That is completely unreasonable! Yet, millions of women ask themselves to do that every day.

"What's the Big Deal about Self-Care? I Don't Think I Really Need It."

Lots of moms (but certainly not all moms) fall desperately in love with their babies, tempting them into a state of needlessness. We adore this new creature and feel fulfilled by caring for them. We need for nothing. This is an illusion. Usually this happens while swimming in an ocean of hormones. We all have needs. Eventually this feeling recedes, and if we abandon self-care, we surface feeling utterly haggard.

In other cases, we feel torn between quality time with our babies and time for ourselves. "I really want to go to yoga, but I feel so guilty being away from my girls," "I went to the library to read my book and I kept thinking how much I just wanted the baby there with me," or even "I know how helpful physical therapy would be for me at this point, but that takes away from the little time in the evening I have with my kids," are all phrases I hear in my office regularly. The truth is, sometimes pursuing self-care is not easy. Sometimes it is its own sacrifice. While we feel nourished by time on our own, we simultaneously miss our babies. We are wired to feel this way. It is evolutionarily advantageous for us to feel this way. However, this does not mean that we are supposed to spend every waking moment with our babies. Stepping away for periods of time to focus on ourselves is a vital practice that we do not want to erode.

"You cannot serve from an empty vessel."

—Eleanor Brownn, author

This is the very essence of why moms need self-care. We are the vessel from which so much pours. Love, care, attention, knowledge, connection, nourishment, and safety are all expected to pour from us to support our children. The more depleted we are, the less there is to pour. Lack of self-care leads to burnout "from a job that you can never quit," Sheryl Ziegler explains in her fabulous book, *Mommy Burnout: How to Reclaim Your Life and Raise Healthier Children in the Process*. We will hear much more from Sheryl as we discuss friendships and connection.

Self-Care Reduces Suffering, Not Pain

The job of a mother is spectacularly fulfilling. But it can also be very difficult. Self-care makes motherhood less hard, but it does not make motherhood easy. With your possible recent experience of contractions, you know there is no avoiding certain types of pain. Labor pains, pregnancy-related symptoms, and sleeplessness are inherent to the process of having a new baby. Elements that are not necessarily inherent to motherhood (resentment, martyrdom, and self-neglect) show up when we disregard self-care.

There is a well-known Buddhist tenet that pain is inherent to life. It cannot be entirely avoided. When living a full life, we encounter pain. We stumble and fall. Loved ones die. Pain happens. Suffering is different though. Suffering is what happens when we resist pain. Sleeplessness and fatigue are inherent to the new mom experience, but our refusal to ask for or accept help with overnight care creates suffering. No one benefits from our suffering. We need to ask for help and do those things that allow us to take care of ourselves. Resenting others for not prioritizing our needs is not productive—it just makes things worse.

Build a Village

In writing this book, I was tempted to slip into a superwoman mode familiar to moms. While many of the topics included in this book are close to my heart, others are beyond my expertise as a psychotherapist. I felt utterly overwhelmed. Then, while interviewing Linda Shanti McCabe, psychother-apist and author of *The Recovery Mama Guide to Your Eating Disorder Recovery in Pregnancy and Postpartum* for my podcast, *Momma Bites!*, she drew a parallel between eating disorder recovery, managing motherhood, and writing her book, saying "the more I asked for help, the better it went." I needed a village. Just as moms need help and support when it comes to tak-ing care of ourselves, I needed to ask for help as well.

Thus began an invigorating and humbling journey to connect with a roster of experts willing to grant me their time and knowledge. Excited to support the message of self-care, each woman offered her own expertise and personal story. Nearly every expert in this book is a mother. All of them felt moved by the challenges of motherhood. It seemed only fitting in writing a book that urged readers to build a village of support, that I assemble my own village. There is no need to suffer alone.

Pick a Lane

A client once referred to me as her "self-care guru." It was one of the greatest compliments of my career. Obviously, I take self-care very seriously. That said, there is no perfect version of self-care. In fact, trying to perfect self-care is the antithesis of self-care (trust me, I've tried and it only drives you crazier). This book presents mommas with a variety of self-care possibilities. They each take time and prioritization, so it's not necessary to use all the self-care opportunities listed in this book. As busy moms, especially new moms, we have to choose lanes. It's about knowing when you need to steer in a particular direction. Maybe you need to focus on breastfeeding for a while, but then later pelvic floor recovery will need your time. Maybe you will start your efforts on finding enjoyable exercise, which leads into finding your way back to your sex life. Throughout our postpartum journey, we need to choose our focus. We cannot be everything to everyone, even ourselves. Jump around in the upcoming chapters. Come back to this book over and over as support for self-care. But never use it as evidence that you're not doing a good enough job at it.

This book is an offering for you. It is not the authority on nursing positions, or whether you should co-sleep, or when to introduce solids. It is a touchstone reminder that, as much as anyone, you need care. I want you to think of this a resource that accompanies you on the wild ride of the postpartum year. Bring us (me and all the moms in this book) along with you to the park, on that first holiday visit to your in-laws, and while you are sitting at Panera wondering how you can eat the soup you ordered while nursing a hungry baby.

Notes

Brownn, Eleanor. www.eleanorbrownn.com, last accessed January 16, 2019.

Shanti McCabe, Linda. "Linda Shanti McCabe: Recovery Mama." Interview by Corinne Crossley and Jessica Foley, *Momma Bites! podcast,* June 26, 2019.

Silver, Emily. "Building Your Postpartum Village: Baby Nurses," interview by Corinne Crossley, *Momma Bites! podcast*, February 2020.

Chapter 1:

Put Your Oxygen Mask On

Self-Care for Your First Postpartum Month

Welcome to your first postpartum month. Consider the next several weeks like a scuba diving expedition. Down is up. Up is down. Night is day, and so on. So goes my speech for nearly every new mother I see in my therapy practice. Based on an epiphany I had in my first week with my new baby, I realized I spent more hours awake in darkness that week than in most of my adult years. I paced our living room, woozy, both desperate and scared to sleep.

Like so many mothers, the cliché for me held true; from the moment my first child was born, life was profoundly altered. Never in my lifetime had I loved so deeply, felt so vulnerable, or experienced such overwhelming emotion. In the midst of my adoration, I stumbled around in the dark, both literally and figuratively. As I peered over at the gorgeous creature in her bouncy chair, the metaphor of scuba diving took hold. I thought about divers jumping into the ocean, no sense of what lay beneath the surface. Early into their descent, the landscape becomes dark and exotic. It can be hard to see, and especially difficult to breathe.

Scuba diving is an adventure—so is motherhood. In both cases, it takes nerves of steel *not* to freak out. As with swimming around in dark depths, there are times when we start to panic and think *What have I done?! I can't handle this! Get me out of here!* Staying calm and curious is the ultimate tool for scuba divers—overreaction yields dangerous effects. Likewise, curiosity and self-compassion are the ultimate self-care tools for new mothers.

What You've Just Been Through

It's no wonder our world feels upside-down—we've just been through the most instantly life-altering experience of our existence. Pregnancy is a head-trip of our bodies feeling out of our control. Then at the end, a baby comes out. Totally wild!

For some women, birth is an empowering experience. They cradle their babies and want to shout from the mountain tops "Look what I just did!!!" But we should not assume this is the norm. Many moms feel exhausted or even let down by their birth experience. We might judge decisions made in the moment, that we now wish had gone differently. Maybe unplanned medical interventions happened for the safety of our baby or ourselves. Or perhaps it just didn't feel how we thought it would. Whatever the expectations you had for birth, I promise you, no one's experience is exactly as they plan. This first lesson in parenthood is a difficult and most apt one. Get comfortable with the unexpected.

For some women, this disparity between expectation and reality results in a need to grieve the birth story they expected rather than the one that happened. This type of grieving (or acceptance work) can be difficult for moms, even when we birthed a healthy baby. We tell ourselves *I shouldn't be feeling this way, everything turned out fine in the end,* yet we still feel traumatized. Paradoxically, acknowledging our feelings moves us toward acceptance.

This was a major feature of the postpartum therapeutic work for one of my fabulous clients. Cecelia was an overachiever. When I met her, she was on the fast track to becoming a director at her job in corporate finance. Whatever she set her mind to, she achieved. This was a major feat since she came from limited financial means and was the sole English speaker in her household as a child. Cecelia's pregnancy was the stuff of fantasy. She was minimally sick, and only struggled a bit with fatigue in her first and last trimesters. Naturally anxious, she shared many concerns about life changes with a new baby, but a difficult birth simply was not on her radar. Yet after days of labor and developing frightening symptoms, it was decided she would deliver via cesarean section.

This was a vastly different experience than she prepared for, being unable to hold her baby or move in the way that she planned for weeks. Healing required giving herself injections and remaining prone for hours—something she was unaccustomed to, even in pregnancy.

"I had no idea how hard and long this recovery would be," she said at our first session in my office since birth. "I feel horrendous and it's hard with so many setbacks. I've had infections, I'm in pain, and I feel totally ill-equipped to deal with this baby."

"Of course, you feel terrible—this was major surgery, and recovery!" I remind her.

"I just thought it would be faster. I didn't know anyone who had a c-section. I had no idea how different it would be."

Allowing herself to heal and manage her pain was a struggle for Cecilia. It was difficult for her to let go of her unrelenting standards and steer clear of comparing herself to her friends who recovered faster. She also needed therapy to grieve her experience of birth and her early days. While she remained deeply grateful that her son arrived healthy, she needed the space to talk about her emotions and body experiences without someone constantly reminding her how lucky she was that her son was fine.

Throughout our work in therapy and her efforts to allow herself a variety of emotions about the birth, Cecilia created room for her entire experience, regardless of whether it made sense. Slowly, she healed both physically and emotionally—but only after giving herself space to soothe both types of pain.

A traumatic birth experience is one of several risk factors for postpartum depression. If you find yourself struggling with these feelings, do not delay in reaching out to a therapist who specializes in postpartum mood disorders. Consult Chapter 7 (page 117) on postpartum mood disorders as well as the Resources section on page 229.

What Is Happening to My Body?

"I firmly believe mothers who have just had babies should be treated like newborns. Mothers and babies both need support, care, food, and sleep. We're the same as our babies."

—Emily Silver, NP, co-owner of Boston NAPS, Infant Care Company

It is late morning within the first few days of bringing my second baby home and I am staring at the shower floor thinking *well, that is definitely the size of a plum, but is it smaller than a peach?* as I watch a blood clot slip down the drain. Just days before, I listened intently as my midwife ran through postpartum recovery information/pep talk. Her jaunty tone did not match my internal alarm with her statement, "Any blood clot bigger than a peach, give us a call." All I could think of was *Peach? Good lord! Conventional or organic?* (It was the end of August and I'd eaten a lot of fruit that summer.)

Even the most basic recovery elements in the early days of your postpartum year can be a bit surprising. The bad news is you will probably be in some discomfort for a while. Your body will do some weird stuff. The good news is this portion of your postpartum era is an excellent boot camp for paying attention to your body and taking your self-care seriously. After all, you *just* had a baby!

Respect the pain. Pain is a highly individualized experience. Modern medicine continues to struggle to understand pain. Pain is complex. Our experience is not simply of pain, but also our feelings about the pain. Post-birth pain is different for each woman and is especially dependent on our birth experiences. Moms recovering from a tear or a c-section have different pain than moms healing from a vaginal delivery. Past incidents of trauma are additional facets of our pain experience. Whatever your individual experience is of pain, respect it.

With this caveat, here are some helpful guidelines.

- Pain should get better, not worse. If your pain worsens, you are going in the wrong direction. If you suspect this is due to increased exertion, slow down. If not, contact your doctor.
- Post-birth pain is likened to a bad period. Your uterus is returning to its previous size, now that it no longer has a passenger. This process involves contractions and resembles period-related cramping.
- Manage pain by keeping your bladder empty, taking medication as prescribed, breastfeeding often (though this sometimes increases contractions), and engaging in light movement.
- Use prescribed stool softeners as directed, especially if you are recovering from a tear or a cesarean birth. Eat fruits, veggies, and other sources of fiber, and drink water to prevent constipation.

- If you are recovering from a c-section and need to cough or laugh, hug a pillow to your abdomen.
- Apply cold packs to hemorrhoids for twenty to thirty minutes to ease discomfort.
- Consult your doctor or midwife about sitz baths to help manage soreness.
- If you did not steal enough of those cooling pads from the hospital, they are now available online.

Respect the bleeding. American culture treats menstrual and even post-birth bleeding (called lochia) as inconveniences to be managed. From our first period, we are handed pads and tampons, told to take some Midol for the cramps, and suck it up through three to five days' worth of bleeding. With this established pattern, it can seem ridiculous to think of slowing down for something that looks like the worst period ever. However, consistent with what your doctor/midwife tells you, bleeding will worsen with too much activity. If you rest as much as your body wants you to (which may be different than how much you want to rest), bleeding slows down. Your lochia can be expected to last between two to six weeks (possibly longer for moms recovering from tears or a c-section), so this dance can go on for a while. Moms might be fine all day puttering about their house, then go out for a longer walk, and end up spending the next couple of days changing pads far more frequently than they had before.

Totally normal weird stuff that happens to your body this month:
- Significant body temperature fluctuations—widely accepted to be hormone-related. This is different from fevers. With any fever, contact your doctor immediately. This can be a sign of infection.
- Passing the biggest blood clots you've ever seen (as long as they are smaller than your fist)
- Rock-hard breasts when your milk arrives
- Tiredness (again, you just had a baby)

Stuff to call your doctor about:

- Bad-smelling discharge
- Passing a blood clot larger than your fist (or a peach)
- Fever
- Chest pain or breathing difficulties
- Severe headache
- Painful lump in your breast
- Red streaks on your breast
- Confusion
- An urge to hurt yourself or your baby
- Chills or clammy skin
- Discharge or pain that gets worse, rather than better
- Severe pain
- Pain, swelling, or warmth in your legs
- Severe bleeding
- Dizziness, altered vision, difficulty seeing
- Pain in the right upper belly or shoulder
- Vomiting or significant nausea
- Rapid weight gain
- Swelling in the hands, face, or legs
- Sadness or negative mood that does not abate
- Twenty-four hours without sleep when provided with opportunity to sleep

Let's Talk Boobs

"Sorry to have to bother you," Mary whispered as she wheeled in her blood pressure machine. "How's it going in here?" she asks, bending over my son's plastic hospital bassinet.

"I think he's doing fine. He's been really quiet. But I just had the craziest, most vivid dream in my entire life. I know I couldn't have slept very long but it seemed like the dream lasted forever."

"Maybe your milk is coming in," she offered, taking my arm.

"Wait, what? Is that a thing?"

"For some people, it is. They report very vivid dreams just as the milk is coming in."

I thought back to the day my milk came in the first time. It arrived abruptly. I went up to my bed for a nap while my parents visited. I went to sleep with my normal breasts. I awoke sweating with rocks where my boobs once were. I couldn't recall a particular dream on that afternoon, but the shock of my body changing so quickly likely blasted that element out of my memory.

"Isn't that a little fast? My milk didn't come in until I was home last time."

"Sometimes it comes earlier if it's not your first," she replied, peeling back the corner of my top. "Yup, your milk came in. Do you want to try feeding him?"

So, it begins . . .

I don't think it is possible to adequately prepare new moms for the first week of nursing. It can be both grueling and inspire a huge sense of accomplishment. Black-and-white portraits of radiant mothers feeding freshly washed infants decorate even the most woke lactation websites. In those early days, it's bullsh!t. I have yet to meet the woman who did not struggle with some element of nursing at some point. In the villages of the past, we witnessed nursing and knew who to reach out to if we had trouble. We would be familiar with the myriad of holds and tricks to help a baby latch. We may even know the stories of women who simply could not nurse, for a variety of reasons, and the resources they used to keep their babies fed.

Remember, this book is centered on your self-care. For a nursing mom obsessed with her boobs, milk supply, and anxiety of whether the baby has enough to eat, some basics are helpful. For more information on lactation and taking kind care of your new knockers, consult Chapter 4 (page 59) on breastfeeding or one of the additional resources listed in the Resources section on page 229.

Fed is Best

We are so privileged to live in a place and time with options for feeding our babies. Some moms choose to nurse. Others opt for formula. For some moms, ending nursing (or never pursuing it) can be a difficult decision. Feeding trends fluctuate wildly, currently arriving at "fed is best." Many moms I know feel that the bottle versus breast debate is often the seed of many mommy wars. They feel judging eyes as they assemble bottles with formula rather than lift the corner of their shirt; others sense glares while nursing their babies.

Fed is best. While other people's judgments hurt, they are not your problem. No one else lives in your body or your life. There is absolutely no need to be apologetic about bottle feeding or breastfeeding. If you decide to move on from nursing/pumping, know that you may grieve. That's okay. Honor it. This is a normal feeling. Each milestone, whenever you pass through it, makes its mark. Create affirmations to remind yourself how beautifully you are nourishing your baby.

Positive feeding affirmations:
- Fed is best.
- Nourishing my baby is all that matters.
- I feel grateful to live in a time where there are options to feed my baby.
- There is no perfect way to feed a baby.

Setting Up Your Feeding Nest

Babies feed a lot. I strongly advise you set up a spot or two in your home for feeding. Get yourself a nice basket or box and fill it with some essentials.

Here are just some ideas:
- Water bottle (insulated if you prefer cold)
- Shelf-stable snacks easily eaten with one hand such as bars, apples and other hand-fruits, nuts, and crackers

- Burp cloths (yes, plural—you will walk away with the one you used last time and forget to bring it back for the next feeding)
- Remote controls (this is where they live until the baby is done with feeding)
- Extra pillows to support your posture
- Books or magazines that sit open on their own

If you have an older child or children, add:
- Activities for other kids
- A few extra snacks for the other kids, because they will want yours from this basket
- Wipes (potty-training children have a special talent for pooping as soon as feeding starts)
- If you have other littles, or someone who will take stuff out of your nest, consider getting a little suitcase or something that closes to minimize thievery.

If you are nursing, add:
- Nursing stool (see below for an explanation as to how it relates to pelvic floor health)
- Cover, if you prefer
- Nursing pillow
- Soothies Gel Pads or other soothing breast pads
- Soothing nursing-approved topical lotion/cream/ointment for nipples (APNO or other topicals)

If you are pumping, make sure to add:
- Pump
- All parts (flanges, tubing, valves, breast cups, membranes, bottles, covers)
- Hands-free expression bra
- Bags
- Sharpie

A PSA for Nursing Stools and Your Pelvic Floor

I bet you skipped right over that one on the list. I didn't have one. *What's the point?* I thought. Being 5'4," to nurse I sat as I do most places: crisscross (since my feet often do not touch the floor if my butt is all the way back in a chair). A bit of a mistake, I learned from pelvic floor specialist Kathy Kates, NP. When I asked her what moms can do early in their postpartum year to start healing their pelvic floor, I was sure she would describe a basic but challenging exercise involving contractions of our nether regions. Nope. It turns out, it is far simpler than that. "Even though you just want to feed the baby when she is crying, take those thirty seconds to make sure your back is supported, that you can feel your sitting bones, your feet are flat on the floor, and that you're bringing the baby to you, rather than the breast to the baby," she listed. If we are under a certain height, a nursing stool may be necessary to keep our feet flat on a surface. Kathy advises, "If you sit on your sitting bones and feet are flat on the floor or on a nursing stool, you're probably up close to where you should be. None of these things happen one hundred percent of the time. The fact that you're thinking about this will make the difference over time."

These Aren't the Feelings I Planned For...

Nursing is not the only thing that can take us by surprise in the first few months of our postpartum year. The realities of our emotional life may vastly differ from our expectations. Lots of women experience a profound difference between how they thought they would feel in this time, versus how they actually feel. This disparity is not our fault. Most every television show, movie, magazine, and social media post sells us images of mothers infatuated with their babies. Sometimes this is our experience, but for plenty of us, it is not. "It's a myth of motherhood that all women instantly fall in love with their babies," says Jessica Foley, a psychotherapist specializing in postpartum mood disorders. "I like reminding moms that they probably didn't fall in love with their partner instantly—why should they expect that with their baby?

This person is a stranger to you, give yourself some time." It is okay to feel ambivalent about your baby.

When I counsel postpartum clients experiencing this, I like to tell them the story of one of my best girlfriends, Rachel. You have not met a sweeter, more baby-obsessed person than she. Rachel was over the moon to be pregnant with her first child and appeared more confident than I could ever imagine at that developmental phase. Finally, her son arrived a few days before Thanksgiving. With the scramble of the holidays, I did not see her until she came home with him. As we stood over her son's bassinet, I studied my friend's sleepy face for that postpartum glow. She looked tired and a bit satisfied, but not in love. "I mean, I'm fond of him," she said, "I'd lay down my life for him. But am I crazy in love right now? No."

I could not have been more surprised and honored by her honesty. Here was a woman who seemed to fall in love with every baby she met, expressing authentic, complex emotions about her own baby. This experience absolutely saved me when I had similar feelings for my second child after being instantly obsessed with my first. This was very hard on me, and had I not seen one of the best mothers that I know go through it, I would have chastised myself about it so much more. You might feel comforted to know that Rachel did fall desperately in love with both of her children. Eventually.

Rest assured if you are experiencing this totally normal developmental postpartum issue, you are not alone. Not everyone has a Rachel in her life willing to be honest about it. Our culture still shames mothers for our authentic ambivalence about our children, even though it should be reasonably expected. That said, the exception to this situation is feelings or urges to cause harm to yourself or your baby. This is a serious and totally different issue which requires immediate intervention from qualified professionals (therapists and doctors). If you find yourself with these types of feelings, contact your doctor and proceed to your nearest emergency room. Do not try to wait these feelings out; they require immediate attention.

Baby Blues

What are the baby blues? How do they play out in real life? Allow me to offer an example from my own experience.

"They just want to drop off some food, I don't know what the problem is here," my husband says, completely befuddled.

"I don't know. I know it doesn't make sense. I ... I ... I just really want to see how the cats get used to her. And she's got this choking thing, I don't know if we need to go right out to the pediatrician. I don't know if I want my sister to come later, and then I don't want a house full of people ... "

"Wait, it's okay for your sister to come over, but not my parents?" I can hear impatience in his voice.

"I don't know. I know it doesn't make sense ..." I stand up from the living room and walk upstairs to close off all the doors forcing our cats to interact with our new baby (I have since learned this is ill-advised). But now I am the one that feels trapped. Cornered. I sense that I might not be in my right mind, but I cannot make it stop. I do not want anyone in this home except my exact tribe—my mother or my sister, no one else. Uncharacteristic for us to argue, at this moment I am not even sure I want my husband here right now.

He follows me upstairs and now we are standing in a claustrophobic hallway. "I'm sorry. I know you want your people here. I'm sure you're frightened too. Seeing her choking like that was so scary. I don't know how I'm gonna sleep while she's doing this or how long it's going to last. That's the only reason why I want my sister to come. It's not that I don't trust your parents. I'm just really, really overwhelmed. I need you on my side. I need us on the same page." Sobs choke my words. I suck in big gulps of air trying to talk. I feel terrified, vulnerable, and completely inept. I feel stupid for feeling this way as a therapist who 'knows better.'

My husband hugs me, but I worry I feel frustration in his posture. I feel torn. I want to be cool. I desperately want to be the chill mom coming home with the baby and settling in. I want to be easy and welcoming to visitors who want to see our little miracle.

Instead I feel more like an animal. I imagine myself holding my baby in a corner of my house, hissing like an angry badger at whomever comes to my door. I have since learned that this is a chemical response, common to many new moms. Even as it happened, I could feel by the outsized nature of the emotion, something bigger than just simple overwhelm taking over my body. My husband's parents are literally two of the kindest people you could ever meet. While on one side I wanted them to see their first grandchild, I also wanted to scream at them to go away.

Despite being a trained therapist working mainly with women, in this moment I had no idea that a case of the baby blues was kicking my ass. In their book *This Isn't What I Expected: Overcoming Postpartum Depression*, postpartum mood disorder specialists Karen Kleiman and Valarie Raskin write: "An estimated 60–80 percent of women who give birth experience a brief, temporary moodiness, sometimes with crying, sadness, irritability, or frustration" (Kleiman & Raskin 2013, 13). These feelings can be "brought on by the coincidence of several major rapid changes: hormone decreases, breast engorgement, and the transition from hospital to home." As they state, these feelings are temporary and different than postpartum mood disorders (further explored in Chapter 7 on page 117). While I knew something beyond my power was ahold of my brain, I could not alter it. All I could do was explain my experience and ask for support.

I tell this story to illustrate a couple of things. First is to show what the baby blues can actually look like. It is all well and good to read a list of symptoms, but until we experience the irrationality, irritability, or reactivity firsthand, it is all theoretical. My husband and I both adore his parents, but something took over my body in those early days where I felt fiercely protective of my baby. Even though it seemed irrational and out-of-hand, it was a totally normal feeling.

I was upstairs with my daughter when my mother-in-law came to the door (my husband had explained via phone that we were ready for food but not visitors). When he started to apologize and explain that we were on the way to the pediatrician's office, I heard her gently interrupt. "No, no, we weren't planning to visit. We just wanted to drop this off in case you were hungry. There will be plenty of times for us to visit soon. Just get settled and let us know how we can help."

They got it.

This is the second reason I tell this story. Ideally, the people you most want in your circle during your postpartum period will get it. They will overlook the crabbiness when you are overtired. They will forgive the reactiveness when you cannot take another piece of advice. They will understand why you cannot handle visitors, even though they just drove through the teeth of Boston rush hour traffic to drop off pasta with pesto and short ribs.

It is painful when those we rely on most (or expect to) do not understand. In these situations, it is important to let yourself set limits. Listen to what your body tells you it needs, whether or not it makes sense. Share your feelings even when they feel ugly and stupid.

Help versus Visitors

"May you always do for others, and let others do for you."
—Bob Dylan, "Forever Young"

A favorite colleague of mine once counseled a client who felt overwhelmed about the impending arrival of her third child. A high-achieving manager in an infamously intense profession, she knew how to assign tasks at her office. Her therapy with my colleague focused on the challenges of asking for help in her personal life. After much working through, this client arrived to session with an answer. Applying some of the same logic of managing employees to gaining assistance with her baby upon his arrival, she made laminated lists to hand out to visitors who said "How can I help?" without the pressure to think off the top of her head. When the question arose, she handed them the list, gave an appreciative smile, and said "anything on this list," before she went upstairs to take a nap or nurse her baby.

I love this story. It is far too often that we struggle to accept the help of others and yet it is entirely necessary in the postpartum year. Help comes in a lot of different forms. Many moms default to family members or close friends for assistance. With this in mind, it is important to make some distinctions here. Let us talk about the difference between a visitor and a helper.

Visitor (vis-i-tor) *noun*: someone who stops by to see you and/or your baby. Visitors may have expectations of what is permitted on their visit (holding the baby, seeing you open a gift, hearing your birth story, giving advice) that may or may not be in line with what you need.

Helper (help-er) *noun*: someone who comes to your home or other designated meeting place with the intention of taking direction to assist you. Potential tasks include grocery delivery, baby holding, entertaining older children and/or needy pets.

Okay, so these are not exactly the definitions you find in Merriam-Webster's dictionary, but I like these better. People often say they want to come by and help, but if you do not feel they will be helpful while you're at your most vulnerable, they are not a helper, they are a visitor. Helpers do not have to be perfect. They just have to take direction, and you need to give it. To help your helpers, the best thing you can do is provide ways to help. Make a list of tasks (or times of day) when support would be helpful.

People cannot read our minds or anticipate our needs. Even your sister who knows you best and has three kids cannot necessarily predict exactly what you need. This can be difficult for any mom to accept, but especially those among us who are perfectionists. In that state (which can be exacerbated by baby blues and postpartum mood disorders) many of us default into an all-or-nothing mindset. Some trademark phrases of perfectionist moms include "never mind, I'll do it myself," or "I'd let him/her/them do it, but I'll just end up fixing it myself," "I know how I like it, so why bother asking for help?" I get it. Sometimes I get sucked into this mindset too. But this year of babyhood is a long haul. Letting other people help in imperfect ways is a skill set. Let people fold your laundry incorrectly. A counter covered with clean dishes is a sign of an empty dishwasher. And for God's sake, this is not the time to worry about how many carbs are in the casserole your neighbor brought over.

Then there are those situations where we do not have access to help. We have a fractured relationship with our families, or our social circle does not include those who want to help out. Or simply, we are a lot more comfortable hiring someone to lean on, rather than dealing with the potential other quid pro quos of asking for assistance from certain folks in our lives. In those cases, there are professionals waiting to help. Here are just a few resources, with more information in Chapter 2 (page 23) and the Resources section on page 229:

Need help with:	Reach out to:
Nursing, pumping	Lactation consultant
New baby care	Postpartum doula
Knowing that your body is healing okay	Your doctor
Feeling okay to sleep at night/managing	Night nurse/Baby nurse overnights
Keeping things clean	House cleaner
Keeping food in the house	Grocery delivery service/Curbside pickup service
Getting meals	Takeout/Meal train

If you feel that you cannot afford or do not want to spend money on these services but could benefit from them, consider asking your health care provider for contacts who may offer services at reduced rates, or telling gift-givers that money or gift cards toward one of these services is how they can truly help.

Visitor Rules

Hopefully you are forming clearer ideas of the differences between a visitor and a helper. I may give the wrong impression here—visitors can be wonderful. They often bring great stuff and are excited to see your new little one. A few might arrive at once, like your grandparents and your aunt, or the three coworkers you have lunch with every day. Their presence is helpful when feeling isolated or alone with your baby.

The best way to keep visits manageable is establishing limits ahead of time (even just for yourself). By the time someone comes by, you could be totally pumped to see someone who does not require feeding, burping, or changing. That said, this is still your first month. Your body is still healing. Your baby is acclimating to their alien environment. Try not to get over-enthusiastic about the length of a visit and what it entails. If you have a partner, invite them to sit down with you to set guidelines around visits.

Here are some other visitor rules:

Set time limits. You might be the most social of animals, but assume you or the baby will tire quickly. Think about how long you want a person to visit, then subtract thirty to forty-five minutes. Set this as your starting time limit. You can always welcome people to stay longer, but setting guidelines is a helpful place to start.

Set visiting hours. Hospitals have them for a reason. Think about what time works for you, not other people. Feel free to set expectations around fussy times and your baby's rhythms.

Set visitor limits. You do not want to feel obligated to entertain. Keep group sizes small. Consider how many people you want to deal with throughout the course of a day. Again, you can be flexible on this later if you want.

Set activity limits. This idea comes from the helpful visitor checklist in Alexandra Sacks and Catherine Birndorf's book *What No One Tells You: A Guide to Your Emotions from Pregnancy to Motherhood.* "Who is allowed to hold the baby? Are we comfortable with the baby being photographed? Can they post the images on social media? If you're nursing, will you breastfeed in front of other people? Does everyone need to wash their hands before holding the baby?" are all excellent potential questions to consider before someone even knocks on your door (Sacks & Birndorf 2019, 221).

Have an email ready. Even if you do not send it, have an email with the guidelines ready to go or post visitor guidelines in a prominent location. Edit as needed, but at the very least you will not be reinventing the wheel each time someone asks to visit.

Call an audible. In football, calling an audible refers to changing a play at the last second. It is the quarterback's responsibility to be surveying the field, adjusting as needed. The life of a postpartum mom and new baby are always in flux. Being able to change up on the fly is an important skill. Just because you told your cousin she could visit on Thursday does not mean you're in any shape to deal with her when it comes. You can cancel.

Resist perfection. People's expectations should be set accordingly. You are brand new to the baby and vice versa. Be dressed when you answer the door, but leave behind concerns about makeup, a clean house, snuggly baby, or patient mood. Hopefully visitors are there to express their love and excitement. Their judgments about you or your home are immaterial.

For more support or information on boundaries and the evolution of relationships in the postpartum year, flip to Chapter 12 (page 207) on family relationships and friendships.

First Postpartum Checkup

According to the American College of Obstetricians and Gynecologists, there was a recent change to the timeline of these checkups. For years, barring specific issues, women waited six weeks to see their providers. In 2018, the ACOG changed their recommendations to connecting with your provider either via phone or in-person around three weeks postpartum, and then if or as needed in the next several weeks, before a full exam at the twelve-week mark.

Don't be shy about going in. Gather your thoughts. Keep a running list on paper in a place where you know you won't lose it, or on your phone (if you do so, keep it in the notes section where you can access it independent of reception, which is difficult in medical buildings). If there was any time to buy into the adage "there are no stupid questions," this is it. If you find yourself shy about asking something, just remember, at some point you will be up in the middle of the night with the baby, feeling vulnerable and worrying about this symptom/issue again. You'll wish you asked about it then. Do yourself a favor, be brave, take up the time you scheduled, and ask your questions.

Mental Health Evaluation

Don't be surprised if you're handed paperwork in the waiting room where you're circling answers about whether or not you've had thoughts about hurting your baby. Instruments like this survey (called the Edinburgh Postnatal Depression Scale) are designed to help providers find those who need help.

Talk to your provider about your emotions. If you are struggling in any way with your emotions, your provider is the first and best resource for getting additional support. Most OBs and midwives are connected with therapeutic and psychiatric providers specializing in postpartum mood disorders. If you do not feel heard by your provider, it is time to find another one. Postpartum mood disorders are both extremely treatable and a major source of suffering for countless women. That is an inexcusable pairing.

A Few Last Thoughts

Scuba diving requires an oxygen mask. The most clichéd example around a caregiver's self-care is the oxygen mask metaphor. If you've managed to avoid this thus far, it is as follows. On planes, flight attendants must make a speech responding to emergencies. "Should the cabin lose pressure, oxygen masks drop from the ceiling. Put the oxygen mask on yourself first before helping anyone else." Many parents say this would be impossible for them. "How could I put the mask on myself first when I know my child needs a mask on too?" I get it. But, if we can't breathe, we're no help to anyone.

This example is the epitome of self-care. If you want to take care of others, you have to be squared-away yourself. This month is chaos, joy, and craziness. Enjoy what is fun, allow other feelings for what is not. Be gentle. Offer yourself the same kindness you give your baby. You are growing and healing together.

Notes

American College of Obstetrics and Gynecologists. "ACOG Opinion on Redefining the Postpartum Visit." Accessed December 1, 2019. https://www.acog.org/Clinical-Guidance-and-Publications/Committee-Opinions/Committee-on-Obstetric-Practice/Optimizing-Postpartum-Care

Bob Dylan, "Forever Young." Track 6 on *Planet Waves*. Asylum Records, 1973, record.

Kates, Kathy. "Pelvic Floor Health for Postpartum Moms." Interview by Corinne Crossley. *Momma Bites! podcast*, January 2020.

Kleiman, Karen, and Valerie Raskin. *This Isn't What I Expected: Overcoming Postpartum Depression.* Boston: Da Capo Press, 2013.

La Leche League International. "Guide to Breastfeeding." Accessed November 15, 2019. https://www.llli.org/breastfeeding-info/

March of Dimes. "Warning Signs of Health Problems After Birth." Accessed November 25, 2019. https://www.marchofdimes.org/pregnancy/warning-signs-of-health-problems-after-birth.aspx

March of Dimes. "Your Body After Baby: The First Six Weeks." Accessed December 1, 2019. https://www.marchofdimes.org/pregnancy/your-body-after-baby-the-first-6-weeks.aspx

Newton Wellesley Hospital. "Patient Guide to Postpartum Pain Management." Accessed November 20, 2019. https://www.nwh.org/patient

-guides-and-forms/postpartum-guide/postpartum-chapter-2/postpartum
-care-pain-management

Sacks, Alexandra, and Catherine Birndorf. *What No One Tells You: A Guide
to Your Emotions from Pregnancy to Motherhood.* New York: Simon &
Schuster Paperbacks, 2019.

Silver, Emily. "Building Your Postpartum Village: Baby Nurses," interview by
Corinne Crossley, *Momma Bites! podcast*, February 2020.

What to Expect "Your Postpartum Checkups." Accessed December 1, 2019.
https://www.whattoexpect.com/first-year/six-week-postpartum-checkup
.aspx

Chapter 2:

Building Your Village

Finding Support for Postpartum Self-Care

"Something that hit me was that I never ask for help," Angela tells me via phone interview for the *Momma Bites!* podcast. She is the cofounder of Mind Body Barre, a barre studio that delivers tough body-positive workouts. At the time we chat, Angela is exceedingly pregnant with her second baby, rounding the bend on the ninth month of a high-risk pregnancy. "I am so grateful to have my sister and my mom nearby. But still, I don't want to ask for help. With this pregnancy being high-risk, I'm asking for a lot of help. It's been humbling. I had to work toward realizing it's okay to ask for help."

She's not the only one.

New moms need so much help. In the initial months of the postpartum era, most elements of life feel completely overwhelming. On paper, balancing baby care, household care, and self-care look like an easy juggle, but in practice, each entail countless specialized tasks. Lots of moms opt for asking family and friends for much of the support they need. This is a fantastic option in many cases. However, as discussed in the last chapter, this is not always a viable option for everyone. Furthermore, many moms find limitations in the type of support they get from their immediate circle. Very few of us have all the resources we need for our postpartum period.

I know you must be sick of hearing it, but we still need villages. We live farther away from our families and friends than ever in history. This is a travesty to the interconnectedness of our communities. We could live three doors away from a maternity nurse and have absolutely no clue she is there. Instead, we live in a time where we must construct our villages. May you find this chapter to be a plethora of potential helpers for self-care. You won't need every resource in this chapter, but chances are you will need someone on this list.

Postpartum Doula

"Birth is a finite event. It ends," Divya Kumar, psychotherapist and former postpartum doula tells me in our interview for the *Momma Bites!* podcast. "Then you go home with this little human and you're like, 'Okay, where are the grown-ups? Wait, I'm the grown-up? Oh, no!'" As we laugh about this shared experience, she defines the role of a postpartum doula as "someone who helps parents and families with the adjustment to parenthood. It can look a bunch of different ways, depending on what people need. From providing information, options, and support, to letting people know what they can expect. Throughout the postpartum year moms are plagued with anxieties about what is normal and what is not—both for their babies and themselves.

Before you (or your mother-in-law) scoff at this idea, tell me it would not be helpful to have someone other than your pediatrician (who you will not see for another week) to ask about those particular weird noises that your baby makes. Consider that a postpartum doula not only has been down the motherhood road herself (in most cases), she has seen other moms in your spot. Divya perfectly sums up the role a postpartum doula can fill by reiterating this conversation with her father. "My parents are from India, and when I called a lactation consultant after my son was born, I remember my dad said, 'We didn't have these lactation consultants in India.' And I was like, 'No, you had all of the aunties who had nursed all the babies coming in and showing you how to swaddle a baby, or you watched other people in your family doing this before, so it wasn't completely new to you.'" Think of a postpartum doula as the aunt or wise village neighbor that you could call, grateful for her knowledge.

Tasks a postpartum doula can provide:
- Feeding and/or breastfeeding support
- Playing with your older child
- Reaching out to your providers/scheduling doctor appointments
- Emotional support for any and all immediate family members
- Providing evidence-based information around recovery expectations for you
- Attending to baby while you and your partner sleep
- Guidance and support around newborn care
- Parental support

- Household management
- Reinforcement of your parenting values and boundaries (e.g., visitors, aspects of care)
- Meal or snack prep
- Referrals

Tips for finding a postpartum doula:
- Ask your friends or contacts if they used a doula and who it was.
- Talk to your obstetrician or midwife for possible referrals for respected postpartum doulas in your area.
- Inquire about certifications.
- DONA (Doulas of North America) International and CAPPA (Childbirth and Postpartum Professional Association) are two organizations dedicated to training and certifying doulas in their work. See the Resources section on page 229 for their website information.
- International Board Certified Lactation Consultant (IBCLC) is the gold standard of lactation support. For more information on specifics around lactation support and training, consult Chapter Four (page 59) on breastfeeding.
- Inquire about privacy policies.
- Ask a potential postpartum doula if she accepts FSA (flexible spending account) cards. HSA/FSA accounts can be used to defray the cost of a postpartum doula.

Baby Nurse

A baby nurse may sound similar to a postpartum doula, but is different—the major difference being the credentials. Baby nurses are just what they sound like—nurses. They completed study and practice to certify as a nurse. Whereas postpartum doulas center their work on supporting you, your baby, and your family through the initial transition period, a baby nurse's focus is more on the baby. However, baby nurses are part of an increasingly popular trend of concierge support services for you and your growing family through all things postpartum.

Tasks a baby nurse can provide:
- Newborn and infant care (bathing, feeding, changing)
- Overnight support, care, and feeding
- Information or educational support around infant behavior
- Support to parents in treatment of common newborn conditions
- Establishing helpful sleep and feeding practices, especially to maximize sleep stretches
- Teaching you how to pump, maintain your pump, and manage breastmilk
- Breastfeeding support
- Incorporating bottles
- Medical attention for moms
- Maternal mental health assessment and referral to therapeutic provider
- Collaboration with other members of your baby's medical team

Tips for finding a baby nurse:
- Reach out to friends who employed a baby nurse as support and ask for referrals.
- Talk to your providers—doctor, midwife, or even the hospital or birth center staff that you find most helpful about who know to contact to fill this role.
- Inquire about certifications—make sure that your baby nurse is a licensed and registered nurse.
- Inquire about cost (this varies greatly and depends on the services you request).
- Find out if friends and family can give gift cards for care (this is the best shower gift ever)!

Lactation Consultant

Dianne Cassidy, IBCLC and cohost of *The Badass Breastfeeder* podcast, recommends setting up your lactation consultation before even leaving the hospital. It is always easier to access care and support by planning for it before we need it. Such a thing is difficult to predict, but there is absolutely no harm in planning to need support. "I always suggest that mommas see a lactation consultant after they get home from the hospital. A lot of moms figure 'there's going to be someone in the hospital, that will be fine,' but often problems show up when they get home and start settling in. The baby is a few days old, your milk is just coming in, and then you have questions that weren't there three days ago," Dianne advises. It is never too early to reach out for a consultation or at least make a connection with a potential consultant to add to your village.

Conditions helped by a lactation consultant:
- Difficulty with latch or adequate feeding
- Painful latch
- Nipple pain or damage
- Managing engorgement or oversupply
- Chronic blocked ducts
- Mastitis
- Low milk supply
- Concern about baby not gaining weight
- Pumping strategies
- Weaning

Tips for finding a lactation consultant:
- Look for an Internationally Board Certified Lactation Consultant (IBCLC). These providers are highly trained and experienced as a result of their certification. Lactation counselors or educators cannot provide the same level of care.

- Request a lactation consultation while in the hospital, especially if experiencing challenges.
- Ask your doctor, midwife, or birth doula for a referral.
- Consult with your pediatrician for a referral to an IBCLC—they may have one in the office.
- Talk with your friends and close contacts and ask them who they liked working with.
- Many hospitals have breastfeeding support groups where moms can drop in or commit to a short module of support (this is also a great way to meet other moms with babies around the same age as yours).
- Remember that "Health insurance plans must provide breastfeeding support, counseling, and equipment for the duration of breastfeeding. These services may be provided before and after birth," according to healthcare.gov.
- Use the United States Lactation Consultant Association website search feature located in the Resources section on page 229.

How a Lactation Consultation Works

Dianna explains the four essential parts of a lactation consultation: intake, measurement, observed feeding, and interventions.

- **Intake:** "If the baby is sleeping when I get there, we have a few more minutes to talk," Dianne reports. "But usually I try to get as much information as I can prior to going to the house. I ask a zillion questions; knowing the history helps me understand what plays into what happens with feedings."
- **Measurement:** "We will weigh the baby (ideally in just a diaper). By weighing the baby before the feeding and after the feeding, we can see how the baby does at the breast. That gives us a little bit of an idea if they are transferring milk well."

- **Observed feeding:** "If the baby is raring to go when I get there, we start with that. I want to see how mom positions, what she is already doing. I don't come in and say 'this is how you should put the baby on or do this.' I always want to know what they are doing. I want to see the baby's suck, their coordination, and how well they move the milk from the mom."

- **Intervention:** "Learning what an effective feeding looks like is helpful. You want to be able to recognize those things." Education is an important source of support for breastfeeding mothers. Your consultant can have some helpful positions up her sleeve, or possible strategies you don't know about. In addition to education and information, an IBCLC can provide referrals to helpful providers, (e.g., pediatric dentists to deal with a tongue tie).

Don't forget, you can reach out to a consultant at any time. Dianne shares this fabulous story to illustrate. "I had a mom reach out because her baby wasn't taking bottles and she was getting ready to go back to work. With an uncoordinated suck, the baby struggled with the bottle. The mom said the baby breastfed great, so we put her on. She breastfed horribly. She got the milk but I looked at the mom and said, 'Is this how it always is?' And the mom reported thinking it was normal to eat every hour, because she didn't know the difference. Since the baby was gaining weight and growing, nobody questioned it."

For more information on all things breastfeeding and pumping, see Chapter Four (page 59) on breastfeeding.

Pelvic Floor Physical Therapist

Where is my pelvic floor? What is pelvic floor physical therapy? How do I know if I need it? "The pelvic floor is a group of muscles that act as a strong and flexible hammock attaching from your pubic bone to your tailbone, and then side to side into the sitting bones. You can also think of the pelvic floor as a muscular sheath that encloses the pelvic organs and pelvic cavity. The pelvic floor works reciprocally by supporting the abdominal muscles, while abdominal muscles help support the pelvic floor," explains pelvic floor specialist Kathy Kates, NP.

We are often unaware of the pelvic floor until we are leaking urine or feces, notably after a vaginal birth. But how did carrying a baby screw up our pelvic floor? Kathy explains, "When you're pregnant, the relaxin your body emits to allow pelvic muscles and ligaments to stretch and support your ever-growing uterus affects all muscles. Those muscles that you probably never paid attention to before were weak, and since having a baby, now they've stretched. Long after the baby is born, those muscles are still both weak and tight. They're not able to support the bladder after those nine months of supporting the growing uterus."

Conditions helped by pelvic floor rehabilitation:
- Urinary incontinence
- Fecal incontinence
- Uterine, bladder, or rectal prolapse
- Painful intercourse
- Hip, SI joint, or low back pain
- Traumatic birth or birth injury
- Recovery from birth-related tearing

Tips for finding a pelvic floor specialist:
- Talk with your doctor at your checkups, ask for an exam to check your tone, and request a referral to a pelvic floor physical therapist.
- Chat with sources of exercise support, if you receive it—personal trainers, yoga teachers, etc. They could have connections toward healing this vital muscle group in your body.
- Have your friends used pelvic floor PT? Who did they love?
- Consult your insurance company for a list of paneled providers, if you plan on using insurance.

- When interviewing a potential provider, inquire about their certifi-cations and trainings. The American Physical Therapy Association recommends a Certificate of Achievement in Pelvic Physical Therapy (CAPP) or Women's Health Clinical Specialist (WCS) certi-fication as a hallmark of adequate training.

Chiropractor

Chiropractic care is not exactly a new intervention. One of my favorite child-hood errands was attending my mom's chiropractic adjustments and even-tually attending my own treatments from a young age. Many women begin chiropractic care during their pregnancies. Hip pain, sciatica, and other lower back pain are common ailments consistent with carrying a baby human inside our bodies. If you don't already have a chiropractor, they can be hugely helpful to postpartum moms.

Common postpartum conditions treated with chiropractic care:
- Hip or lower back pain
- Sacroiliac (SI) joint pain (often due to birth injury)
- Sciatica
- Neck and upper back pain (common with both breastfeeding and bottle feeding)
- Headaches
- Wrist pain (sometimes called mother's wrist) or carpal tunnel syndrome
- Shoulder, elbow, or arm pain
- Birth injuries such as soft tissue injury resulting from pushing
- Pelvic pain, especially lower pelvic pain (even in cases of c-section, the pelvis may still be unbalanced)
- Adjunct treatment for diastasis recti

Tips for finding a chiropractor:

- Consult your existing village—which of your friends and family members have had positive experiences? What techniques did this practitioner use?
- Ask your providers—doctors, midwife, lactation consultant, etc.
- Certain chiropractic schools have search functions to find students trained in their approaches.

Dr. Andrea Wuotila, DC, co-owner of Easton Health Solutions in Easton, Massachusetts, advises the following points as you search for a chiropractic care provider.

- Check out their credentials. Search your state's licensing board to see if a potential provider has any formal complaints filed against them. Formal complaints must be investigated. Yelp and other online reviews are notoriously unreliable.
- Inquire about their treatment approach.
- Explain your pain and ask them how they would approach this issue.
- Ask them about their experience working with postpartum patients.
- Find out what techniques they use. If you are dealing with wrist or ankle pain, make sure to ascertain whether your potential provider adjusts extremities.
- Pay attention to whether you feel like they listen to you. If you feel like they do not, move on.
- Notice how much time they have to meet with you. Some offices book time tightly, so take note if you feel rushed.
- "Find someone you feel comfortable with," Dr. Andrea implores, "because they're putting their hands on you, you need to feel safe and like your needs are being met. As women, we sometimes say 'well, I feel bad if I don't go back . . . ' but if they're a professional, they're going to understand and they're not going to take it personally. Don't be a pleaser—it's about you."

How Chiropractic Treatment Works

How does it actually work? If you have never been, it may feel mysterious. "Consider your body as a self-healing organism that just needs some assistance," Dr. Wuotila illustrates. "Our whole goal is to balance the body and the nervous system as much as possible. We want to put the patient's body into a state where it can just heal itself. That's really our goal in doing spinal adjustments—taking pressure off neurology, getting soft tissue to calm down. It affects the whole body, all your organs, everything. In chiropractic school we are taught the body knows how to heal itself. We're there to facilitate the process.

"A major misconception is that moms have to wait a certain period of time after having the baby before having an adjustment, but you really don't," Dr. Wuotila advises. "If you have a c-section, you have to wait for everything to heal up, but we can still work on your neck or upper back, and make certain accommodations as needed. You can start as early as you want after having a baby."

Initial assessments discuss your physical experience and reasons for referral. At each visit, the doctor examines you on any variety of specialty chiropractic exam tables. Some tables are motorized and start in a standing position, slowly descending you into a face-down position. All chiropractic tables are adjustable and are a major feature of the treatment. Some chiropractors include massage in the adjustment process in addition to physical manipulation of the injured area.

"Moms are so focused on taking care of the baby, we can forget that we have a lot of these aches and pains that worsen. It's better to attack them in the beginning so the whole first year can be more successful around self-care," Dr. Wuotila explains. "New moms come into my office looking exhausted. Here they get to lie down, and have someone providing care for them to feel better with gentle physical touch." Do not underrate how helpful this type of touch can be for your healing process, including your mental health.

Finding the right chiropractic techniques for your recovery will be up to you. "There are so many different ways to treat somebody and that can be confusing as a patient. Some treaters only adjust certain areas of your body, other provide full spine adjustment. Some doctors adjust with instruments or tools. Some people love that, while others want hands-on touch. Regardless of the technique, the biggest thing to consider is whether you are getting results. Do you feel this is worth your time? Chiropractic care is amazing but it has to be the right adjustment for the right person. It is very individualized," Dr. Wuotila reminds us.

Expect to schedule several follow-up appointments about once per week, depending on severity, as your body heals under the direction of a chiropractor. You may be assigned stretches or core-stabilization exercises to supplement adjustments. These appointments are generally shorter in length and move further apart with recovery. Eventually, the goal is to move from a chronic treatment model toward a preventative maintenance schedule.

Acupuncturist

Eek! That's the one with the needles, right? Right. If we're talking acupuncture, we need to talk needles. In my own experience, despite being rather uncomfortable with hypodermics, my desperation to get pregnant pushed me into the Bubbling Brook Acupuncture office. As Suzahne held up a tiny, wire-looking object, she flicked the end to show its size and flexibility.

"That's it?!" I asked, astonished.

"That's it," she nodded.

Two kids and seven years later, while interviewing Suzahne for the *Momma Bites!* podcast and this chapter, I again find myself asking her about needles. Suzahne Riendeau is a licensed acupuncturist and professor of acupuncture in Cambridge, Massachusetts. "People are afraid of pain—that's a number one concern of clients. We use tiny, very flexible, single-use sterile needles. Often, people won't even feel the insertion. People report feeling buzzing, warmth, or flushing—that's what we're looking for. It's all about being comfortable with what's being done. It's never something where you're cringing or not looking forward to it," she reassures.

Postpartum conditions treated by acupuncture:

- Low milk supply or difficulty with let-down
- Hormone regulation
- Birth injuries
- Other chronic injuries
- Pain
- Slow healing
- Sleep problems (other than a baby that will not sleep)
- Adjunct treatment for postpartum mood disorders
- Immunity improvement
- Digestive issues
- Adjunct treatment for organ prolapse

Tips for finding an acupuncturist:

- Reach out to friends and family members for referrals.
- Consult the "find a practitioner" function on the website for the Acupuncture & Oriental Medicine society (acusocietyma.org).
- Consult other providers for referrals.

When interviewing a potential acupuncturist, consider asking:

- How many hours did you train? The answer should be several thousand hours. An acupuncture degree is a four-year, full-time degree.
- What methods do you use? There are many different treatment approaches including non-insertive acupuncture, cupping, and scraping, as well as countless other methods. Set boundaries on treatments that you are not ready to explore.
- "Medical acupuncture" is a catch-all term meaning different things in different places. For example, a medical acupuncturist may be a medical professional with another type of licensure who has pursed acupuncture as a continuing education pursuit, versus a full degree in acupuncture.

- Trust yourself and do not settle for just anyone. Suzahne assures, "You need to have a good relationship with your practitioner. If you're not comfortable, that doesn't mean they're not a good practitioner, it just means that they might not be for you. There are many acupuncturists out there, so there's one for everyone." This treatment is best received in a relaxed state—find someone you trust.

What to Expect in Initial Session and Ongoing Treatment

My first session with Suzahne was like an interview about my body and its function. Reading over the extensive form she assigned me, she asked about everything from headaches, exercise, and what foods I liked, to my baseline body temperature and the quality/color of my poop and pee. Several times during the session I responded, "Jeez, I'd have to think about that, I've never considered or paid attention to that before." I focus on bodily experiences a lot. But the way my acupuncturist asked these questions, I felt a bit out of touch. "We look at all systems in the body, so the first session is spent talking about the issues as well as lifestyle, diet, digestion, breathing, temperature, and sleeping—we're trained to look at the whole person for treatment. I ask questions that a patient might not consider relevant to what they are coming in to be treated for. Then after all that comes treatment," Suzahne confirms.

Treatments may be done sitting in a chair or recliner, or lying down. "The first treatment is based on some fundamentals—pulse quality (I take the person's pulse on several areas of their body) and palpation on the body, especially on the abdomen. I get a lot of information which helps me decide what kind of treatment I need to do for that day. This is really different for people used to a fifteen-minute doctor appointment. Sessions are an hour long with a lot of attention," Suzahne explains.

Each time I met with Suzahne, the treatment was a little different. The week I was well-hydrated differed from the session I came in stressed and running late. One treatment focused on hastening my period to improve flow, while others centered on digestion. While these treatments sound unrelated to another, they shared a common goal. "The oriental medical approach is all about patterns," Suzahne explains, "so we don't try to boil it down to symptoms, so much as look for patterns. Patterns present in many different ways. Two different clients may present with the same symptom of a headache, but the headache is for completely different reasons. It's really important to look at the pattern so we can address the fundamental issues. For new moms, many of their health concerns are about recently giving birth or their postpartum situation, but they also have general health patterns that were there before the baby.

Why Acupuncture?

What is different about acupuncture? Why is it worth it to carve out an hour of time to lie on a table while someone needles you—literally? "When acupuncturists focus on the whole client, we see areas of strength and challenge for each person. Once we help a patient get everything functioning well, the constellation of symptoms bringing them to treatment resolves. Fundamentally in Chinese medicine, the focus is toward being moderate (not too tight, not too loose, not too cold, not too hot). Getting people into that middle ground and staying there without treatment is the goal."

When you pursue acupuncture treatment, you may end up with homework. Little Band-Aid-looking magnets, mini-needles, or press balls have been stuck to my ears, ankles, and wrists. Acupuncturists prescribe these to extend treatment. These are all easily removed and thrown away after use.

Acupuncture for Babies

When I chatted with Suzahne, she reminded me that she treats babies alongside their mothers. "I like to have clients bring their babies with them to treat them together," she explains. "Either moms or babies may present with an issue. They sit together in a chair, lie on the table, or do whatever they need to do to be comfortable. There's no separation between the two of them. We notice that once the baby starts to feel better, the mom starts to feel better and vice-versa. We focus treatment on the baby's back, fingertips, toes, or face. I like to teach moms how to treat their babies. Treating a child is simple—so why not have mom do it? I don't use needles on infants or children under age seven. I use non-insertive tools for stimulating points on the skin and for a short amount of time."

Infant conditions potentially alleviated by acupuncture:
- Premature birth conditions such as mild respiratory issues
- Rashes or skin problems
- Digestive issues
- Colic

Massage Therapist

"But what if I told you that postpartum touch actually is a necessity? Daily touch can often be the difference between surviving and thriving, the difference between depression and connectedness."

—Kimberly Ann Johnson, *The Fourth Trimester: A Postpartum Guide to Healing Your Body, Balancing Your Emotions & Restoring Your Vitality* (Johnson 2017, 166)

What postpartum mom is going to turn down a massage? Plenty of us. We muscle around our car seats, stiffen up during nursing sessions, and walk the floor with uneven hips and shoulders. "I don't have time for a massage," "I can't afford something luxurious like massage therapy," or "I can't lie face down and risk slowing down my milk while I'm nursing" are all excuses for not pursuing this form of self-care. Marketed as the stuff of luxury, massage can be relegated to spas and deemed the ultimate extra. However, with this perception, we miss a source of healing and self-care far more necessary than a pedicure or haircut.

For help understanding the vital role of massage therapy, I reached out to Joy Rober, LMT, in Randolph, Massachusetts. Beyond massage, Joy is certified as both a personal trainer and Pilates teacher. If there is something to be understood about functional movement, Joy is on it.

Why massage?

Joy explains, "I find massage extremely helpful for the postpartum era for a number of reasons. During pregnancy and birth, we change so much. By the time we make it to the postpartum period, where we think our bodies are and where they actually are often don't align. When moms come in during the postpartum time to get a massage, the feedback of somebody gently manipulating things in their bodies allows that mental connection to realign. For example, some people report their legs feel longer as they have a massage. In reality, they did not realize how tight certain areas in their bodies are because it happened in a process over a long period of time. Massage is a way to get back the connection that you've lost through the process."

How can massage help?

Even with attempts to make conscious movement, we fall into habits. "Carrying your child and diaper bag, lugging the car seat, breastfeeding, side sleeping; all these things result in your shoulders rotating forward," Joy explains. "Once they've rotated forward, your chest muscles are in a shortened state. Using shortened muscles to lift or grab something results in them fatiguing fast. Massage therapy to help gently open these shortened muscles begins reversing this pattern. This can even be done if you're breastfeeding."

Postpartum conditions treated with massage:
- Sciatica
- Neck, upper back, and pectoral pain (consistent with hunching in breastfeeding positions)
- Hip misalignment
- SI joint pain
- Carpal tunnel syndrome

- Shoulder pain
- Decreased grip strength

Tips for finding a massage therapist:

- Ask friends and family members who they recommend.
- If you are seeing a chiropractor or physical therapist, consider asking for local referrals.
- Tune in closely to how you experience the atmosphere of the office. If you do not feel comfortable, allow yourself to leave or end a session at any time.
- Chat with front office staff and let them know if this is your first massage, especially if you are feeling anxious about the experience or provider.
- Inquire about the massage therapist's prior experience treating similar symptoms as well as postpartum bodies.
- Pay attention to whether you feel heard and listened to.
- Remember, you can end the session at any time. No treatment is one-size-fits-all. Massage is not for everybody.
- Notice whether the massage therapist supports you in your choices rather than inviting you into guilt (for example, if you wish to keep certain clothes on during your massage). If a massage therapist cannot adapt to your needs, they are not the right therapist.
- Massage is adaptable. Everybody is different and each massage is different. Pay attention to the therapist's adaptability.
- If you are experimenting with trying massage or even considering whether a certain massage therapist is the right fit, book a shorter trial session.

What to Expect in Initial Session

You will be asked to fill out a form reviewing your medical history and inventory of presenting issues. Expect to list medications, sources of exercise, and whether you are pregnant. If this is your first massage, make that clear. Let the provider know if you feel nervous or uncertain. If you are nursing, discuss how you want to handle this in treatment (e.g., lying face down or not).

Joy advises, "It's important to find a massage therapist that listens to you. If you're not comfortable before you even get on the table, it is not a good fit. Once you're on the table, you want the massage therapist to be checking in with you. You never want to have a massage where they're doing something and it doesn't feel comfortable, while in your mind thinking, *well, they know what they're doing so I'll just let it happen.* Everybody's different. The massage therapist may apply the same amount of pressure they applied to another person, but it's not a good fit for you. It is always important that you leave the treatment feeling positive."

Basic massage etiquette:
- Inform the provider if this your first massage.
- If helpful, discuss the level of dress that is comfortable to you. If you want to leave your bra and underwear on, be clear about this. This is a completely acceptable request, but it can be helpful to address so that providers also know what to expect.
- Depending on your level of dress, collaborate with providers to get your needs met. Joy explains, "The general etiquette is, if you keep underwear on, the massage therapist won't interfere with that. However, if you're keeping underwear on because you're menstruating, and they need to get to a certain area like if you had sciatica problems, the massage therapist may ask if they can work under the underwear on the area of the glute or hip that is covered. However, if you're uncomfortable with that, they can do compressions even over the sheet. There are many variations and it is all about what you're comfortable with. I've had people keep pants on or remain in a tank top and that's fine. It's all what you're comfortable with. You never know what anybody's past experience has been."

- Speaking up helps the massage therapist understand what is best for you. You are cultivating a trust relationship. Whatever you need is fine and a massage therapist's job is to work with you.
- Most facilities and treatments are based on time (thirty, sixty, or ninety minutes). Remember, that is your time. Talk about and ask for what you want and do not want.

Tips for treatment:

Ongoing treatment focuses on realigning the body. Joy elaborates, "If your structure is out of alignment, your body weight is naturally misplaced. This puts pressure on certain muscles and creates repetitive cycles that go unnoticed until we are in pain. When we say, 'I think I slept funny' or 'I stepped wrong,' a lot of those times, it's not that simple. It's not that you slept funny. Your body was already out of alignment and it got so far out that when you did something, your body decided it was done. We were warned with muscle cramps, tension, and fatigue but didn't listen until pain happened. The sooner you listen to your body, the quicker you get out of unhelpful patterns. Once you get to the point where there is pain, it is a longer process for recovery because your body plays tug-of-war. You've got the front competing with the back, the left competing with the right. Now you've got to calm and address everywhere. Your body goes into a protective mode. If there is an injury, it compensates. That compensation alone can lead to other injuries down the road. Everything is connected.

"With relaxin still present in the body of nursing moms, massage therapists need to be cautious of overstretching already hypermobile ligaments. The job of the massage therapist is helping muscles gently relax, not overstretch. Knowing your beginning range of motion is helpful in this situation. Everyone is different with their automatic range. Moving one or two additional degrees is progress. You want it to be a slow process so you're not overdoing it and overstretching a ligament," Joy continues.

Set your expectations realistically. A single massage is not going to resolve long-standing pain. Joy advises, "Just feeling that it has somewhat diminished is progression—not completely gone, but diminished. If you're leaving and that pain has intensified, then it was not a good experience. Something was overdone."

Do not forget this is a highly physical treatment for the body. Joy states, "As gentle and relaxing as massage can be, it does speed up blood flow. It's a workout for your muscles, even though you're not sweating. Your body is pumping oxygenated blood to former areas of tightness and stress— that's a workout right there."

Drink water and monitor your soreness. "There might be a little bit of soreness, but it should never carry over multiple days. Ideally it would be great if you don't get soreness, but if you do, expect it to last about a day," according to Joy.

Finding a Psychotherapist

For information on adding individual or couples therapy to your support village, turn to Chapter 7 (page 117) on postpartum mood disorders or Chapter 10 (page 181) on relationships.

Additional Logistical Support

Cleaning companies, automatic diaper deliveries, and grocery delivery services are just a few of the creative sources of support in our ever-changing world. If you can afford these services, there is no better reason than what this year presents to validate their helpfulness. Establish accounts. Freeing up time for sleep, movement, time out of the house, or longer baby snuggles is the very definition of self-care.

Notes

Cassidy, Dianne. "Dianne Cassidy, IBCLC, on Breastfeeding and Badassery." Interviewed by Corinne Crossley, *Momma Bites! podcast*, October 3, 2019.

Hawthorne, Angela. "Changing Your Relationship with Exercise." Interview by Corinne Crossley, *Momma Bites! podcast,* February 2020.

Healthcare.gov. "Breastfeeding Benefits." Last accessed December 1, 2019. https://www.healthcare.gov/coverage/breast-feeding-benefits/

International Childbirth Education Association. "International Childbirth Education Association: Role and Scope of the Postpartum Doula." Last accessed November 1, 2019. https://icea.org/wp-content/uploads/2015/12/Role-Scope-of-Postpartum-Doula-3.pdf

Johnson, Kimberly Ann. *The Fourth Trimester: A Postpartum Guide to Healing Your Body, Balancing Your Emotions & Restoring Your Vitality.* Boulder: Shambhala, 2017.

Kates, Kathy. "Pelvic Floor Health for Postpartum Moms." Interview by Corinne Crossley. *Momma Bites! podcast,* January 2020.

Kumar, Divya. "Postpartum Health and Racial Inequity." Interview by Corinne Crossley, *Momma Bites! podcast,* February 2020.

Riendeau, Suzahne. "Acupuncture for Your Postpartum Health." Interview by Corinne Crossley and Megan Mountcastle, *Momma Bites! podcast,* March 2020.

Rober, Joy. "Massage for Your Postpartum Health." Interview by Corinne Crossley, *Momma Bites! podcast,* March 2020.

Silver, Emily. "Building Your Postpartum Village: Baby Nurses," interview by Corinne Crossley, *Momma Bites! podcast,* February 2020.

Wuotila, Andrea. "Postpartum Chiropractic Care." Interview by Corinne Crossley, *Momma Bites! podcast,* February 2020.

Chapter 3:

Changes, Acceptance & Good Enough

Foundational Self-Care Skills

"Arrgh!"

"Do you need help at all?" My twelve-year-old helper pops her head into my kitchen, responding to my guttural sound of frustration.

"No . . ." I say, my irritation apparent. Despite her presence, my baby wants only me. I drop all the baby food–making equipment and switch to a task I can do with him on my hip: unloading the dishwasher. Suddenly he wants to be put down to scoot on the floor. I put him down and he pulls at the racks, toppling over, missing the corner of the appliance's door by millimeters. He collapses crying. I grab him, hoisting him back to my hip, less gentle than I prefer. He cries harder. I hate myself. I hate that I cannot seem to stop the perfectionist machine in my head, insisting on making my son's baby food in the way that I made my daughter's. I hate that I can't put two minutes in a row to get something done. I hate that I'm prioritizing dishes and stupid f!cking baby food over connecting with my kids. I hate all of it. Most of all, I hate myself for hating it.

In many ways, I knew how to take care of myself in my postpartum years, even if just in concept. I am a therapist. I prescribe self-compassion to my clients and wholeheartedly believe in it. But it can be a mind game. When I turned my intentions toward self-kindness, my mind tossed out excuses. *Sure, self-care is important, but don't let that pull you away from time with your kids. Sure, taking time for yourself is good, but what about taking care of your marriage? Of course, she wants me to do what's kindest for myself, but my mom would never say if she felt sad because she was missing me and the kids.* There were so many reasons to throw self-care to the wayside.

The decision to make all of my son's baby food is one I still consider to be the worst choice I made in my postpartum year. I use this example often with clients stuck in beliefs about what 'good moms' do. On its face, a mother making all her baby's food is the stuff of Pinterest boards. People oohed and aahed as I opened stainless-steel containers of pureed zucchini, whipped cauliflower, and berry sauce. *"Oh my God,* you're so good. That's so amazing that you make all his food," people said admiringly. It only furthered their perception of me as a health expert. Sure, I got off on it a little bit. When I fed my daughter the foods I made, it was fun. She was an enthusiastic eater and loved nearly every last morsel I whirred in my food processor. Sometimes exhausting, but overall, it was a source of joy and connection in our first year together.

You know who didn't like homemade baby food? My son. He gagged on the first zucchini I ever fed him. He coughed when I fed him hand-strained green beans. When he could chew, I created cauliflower tots that he ate enthusiastically—once. I didn't know what to do. The best possible care for all of us would be to stop the hours of blending and stirring, but I could not let it go.

I know this sounds insane, but I had my reasons. The truth is, I hadn't expected to fall so headfirst in love with my daughter from the moment she was born. It is the only case where love opened up, swallowed me whole, and left me breathless. This was the only way I knew to have a baby, but it was different with my son. I expected to be spirited away in the same manner, but it didn't happen at first. I adored him, but life pulled at me. I worried my daughter felt like a second-class citizen, and became wracked with guilt when I lost my patience with her as a result of being an exhausted, stressed, new mother of two. He was a good baby, but higher-maintenance than her (probably because he did not have our undivided attention). My worries took the form of irritation and I felt angry more of my postpartum year than I wish to remember.

I felt guilty so much of the time. I worried he didn't feel loved in the way we had loved her. *If I can do all the things for him that I did for her, he will feel loved,* my postpartum brain told me. *You made all her baby food? Make all of his. Remember all the times after dinner that you rolled around playing with her on the floor? Make sure you do that for both of them each night.* Mind you, I attempted fulfilling these standards while remaining unrelenting on the standards of care for my daughter.

My heart still breaks for all of us in that time.

Skewing toward anxiety for much of my adult life, my relationship with change can be tempestuous. One part of me finds excitement in new adventures, while another part prefers to recite all the things that could go disastrously awry. Studying coping mechanisms and my work as a therapist provide me daily evidence that anyone can thrive in change. Alas, we are all human. Having my second baby spun me around. My anxiety got in the way of trusting the skills (flexibility and curiosity) that worked in past life changes, including my first year with my daughter. Instead, I clung to tasks and list items. In change, the more rigid we are, the more it shakes our foundations.

Ch-Ch-Changes

Most of us are hard-pressed to think of a more life-altering experience than having a child. Even if you are just weeks into being a mom, no one needs to tell you how crazy this change is in your life. Rather than focusing on the specific changes you face, it can be more helpful to consider how we deal with change—our change styles. Everyone has a change style. People are complex animals comprised of past experiences, and internalized messages, all influenced by brain chemistry. Years of dealing with change lead up to having a child. Let's take a look at our change styles to see how they work for us—and possibly how to change them.

Styles of change (can overlap or evolve, depending on nature of change):

Anxious: You often dread change, even with things you want. You are a planner. You want plenty of notice to deal with upcoming change, so you can focus on all the elements to forecast or manage. You see countless angles where things can go wrong and are surprised when others do not see a negative outcome happening from miles away.

Resistant/irritable: You feel irritable or annoyed when dealing with change—especially if change is thrust upon you. You feel a lack of control or authorship in managing changes. You feel powerless and ineffective in this situation. You might lash out or isolate as a result of your irritability.

Frozen/avoidant: You feel immobilized when change is thrust upon you. Indecision paralyzes you. Not knowing how to move forward through change leaves you stuck. Often you are only spurred forward by external forces such as time running out, another person's needs, or external consequences. If left to you and your motivation alone, overwhelm threatens to keep you stuck forever.

Flexible/curious: Somewhere in your life you cultivated the skill of curiosity. Even in cases where you are not overjoyed about the changes you face, you allow yourself to be curious where things will go. You identify less with outcomes than ways you can feel effective dealing with change. You are less concerned with how others judge your management of change, instead allowing others' judgments to represent their values rather than your abilities.

Fluid: Your deep curiosity and life experience inform your resiliency. You have acceptance of life's inherent impermanence. Each change presents a fresh opportunity. You are probably a Buddhist monk or yoga guru.

Let's be clear, we are not shooting for fluidity here; we aim for increased flexibility. If reading this leaves you feeling that you have a "wrong" change style, think again. Start with some compassion and understanding about our change styles. Change is hard. If you have an anxiety-based change style (anxious, resistant, or avoidant), that same style probably benefited you in other parts of your life. Those who resist or remain anxious around change are often excellent at jobs that entail discerning detail or predicting outcomes. Just because this style creates struggle in your personal life does not mean it is all bad. Honor your style and thank yourself for the way that it works for you.

Working to evolve your change style requires acceptance. The more we accept our change style without judgment, the more we can work with it. Curiosity promotes acceptance. Acceptance promotes change. In compassionate understanding of how we deal with change, we can work toward flexibility. Take what you learned about your change style to create helpful affirmations. For example, in knowing that I tend toward anxiety when dealing with change, I offer myself the ideas *planning for every possible outcome will make you more anxious, not less. This is your anxiety. Try to be curious and*

trust yourself to handle whatever happens. Take a moment to pause and write some kind, non-judgmental affirmations:

_____

_____

_____

_____

But What If I Don't Want to Accept This?

If you struggle with acceptance, you are not alone. Even people open to change still bristle at acceptance. Don't confuse acceptance with approval. You may worry that the acceptance of something upsetting equates with condoning it. It doesn't. But in our all-or-nothing society, this is an understandable misconception.

Acceptance is closer to acknowledgment. Whether or not you approve of your infant's sleep schedule, you can accept it. Acknowledging that your baby is not sleeping at night and takes a huge nap at 5:00 p.m. does not mean you want things that way. It does not mean you are not addressing this issue. It simply means this is how things are right now. The cliché "it is what it is" epitomizes acceptance.

What's the big deal about acceptance? Acceptance reduces struggle. It helps slow down the negative voices in your head. It provides clarity to see the most viable solutions in the moment. Reducing struggle in the life of a new parent is always a win.

What most gets in the way of acceptance is holding onto our judgments. Too often, we maintain allegiance with our judgments to the detriment of taking effective action. Sticking with judgments prolongs suffering. We cannot move forward effectively without accepting where we really are.

Good Enough Mothering

"What do you mean 'good enough?'" Lila asks when I bring up the topic in session.

"The idea is that you don't have to be perfect. Truly, there is no such thing as perfect—especially when it comes to mothering. We all do it differently. We all have different kids. If we have more than one child, they are different from one another. We cannot mother them perfectly. The idea is not to shoot for perfection, but rather, what is good enough for each child."

"But . . ." Lila pauses, her eyes scanning my office as she processes this idea, "that doesn't sound, well, good enough." She laughs.

I laugh too. "Why not?"

"Because, I should be trying to be better than that for her."

"Better than good enough?"

"Yes! I just love her so much," she says, getting teary, "she deserves even more than that."

"More than a mom who responds to what she needs as she needs it, but not perfectly, resulting in small instances of manageable strife?"

"Well . . . yes?"

The concept of good enough mothering is nearly a century old. The idea stems from research and theories on attachment, most notably by D. W. Winnicott. A pediatrician out of England in the 1930s, Winnicott drew his theories from working with parents and children, as well as his studies in psychoanalysis. Through these observations, he coined the phrase "the ordinary devoted mother" currently known as "good enough mothering." Unlike many of his contemporaries, Winnicott gave moms their due. Winnicott believed the work of motherhood was extraordinarily important and correctly realized it involved a myriad of tasks that were impossible to perfect.

While Winnicott's work dates back to a different era, the idea of the good enough mother applies now more than ever. Because the world is a complex, imperfect place, our children need to see us make mistakes and embody imperfection. Kids should neither expect perfection from others nor themselves. "An imperfect mother helps her child gain the skills to tolerate frustration, become self-sufficient, and learn to soothe himself," Alexandra Sacks and Catherine Birndorf write in their book *What No One Tells You: A Guide to Your Emotions from Pregnancy to Motherhood* (Sack & Birndorf 2019, 196). Pursuing perfection is a setup for disappointment and resentment. Allowing ourselves to be imperfect creates opportunity for us to be present, and resilient.

Also? Being a good enough parent is still a lot of work. Unlike the usual American all-or-nothing mentality, good enough does not mean you zone out in front of your phone for hours not paying attention to your baby. Good enough moms still attend to their kids. However, simply keeping our babies fed and clean today could be the entire agenda for a good enough parent. Other days entail additional items on this list. The criteria to meet the good enough bar changes every day.

Lila took quite a while to wrestle with the concept of the good enough mother. After years of perfectionistic tendencies, it only made sense for her to pursue these same standards in the care of her child. However, during some difficult patches in her postpartum year, she was able to see how these tendencies got in the way of being effective. Despite coming from a place of love, Lila saw when she was stuck in perfectionist mode, she alienated others, worsened her stress, and found it impossible to feel emotionally present. Trying on the concept of being a good enough mother required more challenging skills like (you guessed it) flexibility, curiosity, and acceptance. Lila had to remain flexible and curious as to what her child needed, and accept her own ability to provide it imperfectly.

Lots of moms struggle to create a practice of good enough mothering. Emily Silver, co-owner of Boston NAPS, a baby nurse and parent education company, offers this simple exercise for postpartum moms. "We tell moms when they wake up each morning to say out loud one thing they are going to do for the day, one thing they're not going to do, and one thing they're going to ask for help with. It doesn't have to be big. You could wake up in the morning and say, 'I'm going to take a walk with my baby, not fold the laundry, and ask my partner to pick up dinner on the way home from work.'"

Try it:

One thing I'm going to do today:

_____

One thing I'm not going to do today:

_____

One thing I'm going to ask for help with today:

_____

Go forth and use this. Bring it to your friends. Start a tribe of good enough mothers with reasonable expectations who ask for support. Now those sound like some fun ladies to hang out with!

Good Enough Affirmations

Perhaps with some wider understanding of the concept of good enough mothering, you can craft some helpful affirmations for when you are on strug-gle street. When we most need the good enough approach can be the time we are least in touch with it. Exhaustion and overwhelm predispose us to unfor-giving standards of ourselves (and others). Consider some of the following reassurances that I heard repeatedly from many of my podcast guests and experts interviewed for this book.

You're doing a good job. I know this one is difficult to buy when you are struggling, but it is probably true. If you are keeping your baby fed, trying to get her to sleep, and changing her diapers fairly often, you are doing a good job. If this is too difficult for you to swallow, consider "you're doing the best you can." Even if you think you aren't, you probably are. I know this might be below your standards, but in the postpartum year this is often the best we can do.

You just have to be a washcloth monkey. This affirmation comes from my favorite postpartum psychotherapist, Jessica Foley. She employs the work of Harry Harlow, an attachment researcher who famously conducted experiments with monkeys. Baby monkeys were separated from their mothers, and then provided food by a wire-constructed stand-in mom. Though the monkeys had food, many of them developed failure to thrive and some died. Harlow then, keeping everything else the same, tossed a washcloth over the wire moms, making them more snuggly. The babies thrived. Jessica reminds us, "I really love this concept because the pressure is so high for moms. But when you look at what babies need to thrive, it's not that much. You do not need to be doing everything to the best of your ability, you just need to offer comfort, love, and care."

Asking for help/letting people help is a strength. Letting others help is a gift you give them. Not a sign of weakness. It is a sign of strength, management skills, and being in tune with the trend of villaging.

The "right" way to care for your baby is just theory. Freaking out that you are not doing everything right to cultivate strong attachment? Worried you're not stimulating enough cognitive development in your baby? It's okay. Do the best you can when you can. Our understanding of babies changes over the years. Remember, Winnicott and Harlow's work was considered groundbreaking at the time because people used to think it was bad to hold your baby. Remind yourself even if you did everything perfectly (which would make you and those around you crazy) your baby would still have both strengths and challenges.

In Case of Emergency, Break Glass: Self-Compassion Skills

What's so important about self-compassion? We treat self-compassion as a nice add-on to our lives if we can swing it. We relegate it to the realms of yoga classes or flowers bouquets from the grocery store, but self-compassion is essential throughout the postpartum year (and spoiler alert, all of motherhood). When we find ourselves challenged by something, we rarely offer ourselves the same reassurance we provide others. Instead, we punish and chastise ourselves. *Ugh, why can't I do this today? Other people do this all the time!* or *My baby does not sleep and I am on my second case of mastitis, why do I suck at this?* We think being hard on ourselves spurs us into action, but in fact it does quite the opposite. We end up more overwhelmed, less resilient, and increasingly upset.

What is our way out of this spiral? Self-compassion. Kristen Neff, PhD, author of *Self-Compassion: The Proven Power of Being Kind to Yourself*, and a foremost authority on self-compassion, challenges us to conside that "having compassion for oneself is really no different than having compassion for others. Think about what the experience of compassion feels like. First, to have compassion for others you must notice that they are suffering. Second, compassion involves feeling moved by others' suffering so that your heart responds to their pain (the word compassion literally means "to suffer with") When this occurs, you feel warmth, caring, and the desire to help the suffering person in some way. Having compassion also means that you offer understanding and kindness to others when they fail or make mistakes, rather than judging them harshly. Finally, when you feel compassion for another (rather than mere pity), it means that you realize that suffering, failure, and imperfection are part of the shared human experience." What would happen if you offered yourself the same kindness you offer others? It doesn't make you lazy, complacent, or soft. It makes you more effective and kinder to others. When all other skills prove difficult to implement, use self-compassion. In suffering, it can be a hard thing to turn toward, but I promise you, it is never the wrong thing to do.

Here's a technique I recommend.

Exercise: Self-Compassion Visualization

As a mom, you are now more in-touch with the vulnerability of small children and babies. When stuck in a spiral of self-criticism, call up an image of yourself as a baby or very young child. If helpful, recall a childhood photo or video.

Visualize this picture of yourself in pigtails or a onesie or smiling in a bath. Let yourself feel love for that little person similar to the love you feel for your baby.

Hold yourself accountable for the words you say to yourself. Would you ever say the things that you say to yourself in adulthood, to this little child? Try to imagine that little person and resist saying them to her. You are still that child inside and just as hurt when you say unkind things to yourself.

Notes

Neff, Kristen. "The Three Elements of Self-Compassion." Last accessed November 28, 2019. https://self-compassion.org/the-three-elements-of-self-compassion-2/

Sacks, Alexandra, and Catherine Birndorf. *What No One Tells You: A Guide to Your Emotions from Pregnancy to Motherhood.* New York: Simon & Schuster Paperbacks, 2019.

Foley, Jessica. "Postpartum Mood Disorders: More Than Just the Baby Blues." Interview by Corinne Crossley, *Momma Bites! podcast*, January 2020.

Silver, Emily. "Building Your Postpartum Village: Baby Nurses," interview by Corinne Crossley, *Momma Bites! podcast*, February 2020.

Wikipedia. "D.W. Winnicott." Last accessed October 28, 2019.

Winnicott, D.W. *Babies and Their Mothers.* Boston: Da Capo Press, 1992.

Chapter 4:

Let's Talk Boobs

Breastfeeding

My three-year-old scrunches her face and sucks in air with big gulps. "Ow ow ow ow ow ow!" she says holding her doll to her chest under her shirt. She is nursing her baby. Apparently, this is what nursing looks like to her. This should be no surprise. In the days after her brother arrived, I attempted to breastfeed him the way I nursed her. She was tricky to nurse—literally. She fooled every nurse on the maternity floor, except the lactation consultant who saw she was "on but not latched," whereupon she fell into snuggly sleep. For a month, I stripped her down to a diaper to keep her awake enough to finish feedings. Eventually after some supplemental formula and pumping, we got a rhythm. My nipples chapped but grew a tolerable sensitivity. It was not easy, but I never cried (well, not because of pain).

With my son, it was different. In response to his hungry cries, I would settle us into our nursing nest. My daughter played in her dollhouse or looked up from her read-along books to see fat tears falling from my eyes. In the beginning, it took effort to resist the reflex to strike my newborn whose nursing sent needles of electric shock–like pain through my breast. With each feeding, I urged myself to keep going, thinking *maybe this is the one where it stops hurting so bad*. But it never was. My husband called my doctor's office and begged on my behalf for APNO (short for all-purpose nipple ointment), the one thing that got me through the toughest days of nursing my daughter. The nurses on the other end of the phone reminded him that the prescription had to be mixed by a compounder and may not be covered by our insurance. "I don't care if it costs a thousand dollars and you have to drive out of state," I hissed. "Get me some."

After nearly a week of sobbing at every feeding, I called my pediatrician's office and beseeched them for their soonest lactation consultant appointment. "I'll come any time. I'll bring her dinner if she's staying late for me," I promised, only half kidding. I would do anything for a little help. That evening as we waited in the exam room, outside the sun set and it was getting dark. I paced the small room while my postpartum brain raced. *What if she says it's nothing? What if she says I'm being a wuss and must not remember*

how uncomfortable it is? What if I can't nurse? What if there's something wrong with his suck? My mind was already eager to pin blame or settle on hopelessness for our situation.

"My goodness, have you let down already?" she asked, bustling into the room and seeing the front of my shirt.

"No, he just peed all over me," I said, acknowledging the extensive puddle spreading over the majority of my shirt. I felt embarrassed and even more vulnerable. How could I still feel this inexperienced as a second-time mom?

She laughed and pulled up a chair. After a series of questions, it was time for us to nurse. I presented my milk-swollen breast to my son.

"He looks like he's nursing," she said leaning in to observe, "does it hurt?"

"Ummmm . . ." I started. It hurt. But it always hurt. Did I feel like I had to cry? Was I about to yelp in pain? Not in that moment. "I mean, it usually hurts more than this . . ."

"Let's take a look," she said, popping his suck with her pinky finger and looking at my breast after a few minutes of nursing. "See what's happening?" she said pointing to the shape of my nipple, "He's nursing great. He's getting all the milk he needs but he's nursing on his hard palate, rather than his soft palate. That is fine for him, but really uncomfortable for you."

You can say that again.

Within fifteen minutes of practice wherein I learned to correct his latch, my little guy and I completed our first feeding that did not entail me sobbing. Soon nursing him became special and spectacularly convenient.

Your Lactating Boobs: A Care Manual

It's not as if I did not know that breastfeeding could be difficult. I learned firsthand from my sister's heroic attempts to nurse my niece through three separate cases of mastitis that truly "fed is best." According to the CDC, more than 81 percent of moms attempt to breastfeed. By six months, 51 percent report still nursing, and that number drops to 30 percent by the one-year mark. Breastfeeding is not for everyone. As moms, we are so fortunate to live in a time when breastfeeding our children is just one of the possible options to feed them. Formula is a miraculous innovation of our era. I learned from my sister's slog (told later in this chapter on page 67) that nursing is not necessarily an intuitive exercise. "I don't understand!" she would cry, my niece wriggling with hunger. "Women have done this in the fields for centuries, why is this so hard?" Had it been a matter of will, she would have gotten it in the first hour. But nursing is not a matter of will. Education helps. Classes on holds and what to expect help. Reaching out for support helps. Acknowledging what works and does not work for you helps. For her, it was her iron will that took her through five weeks of nursing before she had had enough. She bravely accepted it was not working for her. It was time to feed her daughter in a way that did not hurt.

Pain & Discomfort

"I've been walking around topless for two days. Too bad if Dave thinks it's totally hot, I can't think of anything that I want less than to be touched right now," Rachel's text reads. I feel lucky to be exchanging messages with one of my best friends on a bright Tuesday morning. We commiserate about the discomforts of early nursing, our babies only ten days apart. "I can't even stand to brush my boobs with my own arm. Ugh, I'm so sensitive, even the air hurts. How can air hurt? How is that possible?"

When I spoke with Dianne Cassidy, International Board-Certified Lactation Consultant (IBCLC) and cohost of *The Badass Breastfeeder Podcast*, she confirmed our need for support and education around breastfeeding. "Education is key when moms run into challenges. One of the first things I address with moms is the pain aspect. Rumor on the street is breastfeeding is painful and you just suck it up until it no longer hurts. The truth is, if nursing is painful the entire time you're feeding, that is a red flag." You heard it from a professional—if you are having pain with nursing, put down this book and call yourself a lactation consultant.

"In those first two weeks, with hormonal changes, labor, and delivery, of course you're going to be tender—but that should last for thirty to sixty seconds. Then you should just feel the tug of the feed. There should not be pain. From day one. Do not get into that place where you're thinking 'oh, it'll get better, it'll get better, it'll get better.' Pain is a sign that there is something more going on."

I urge you to go back to Chapter 2 (page 23) and read about the importance of connecting to a lactation consultant. Lactation consultations are often covered by insurance and can provide life-changing advice, improving your experience in a matter of minutes. Rest assured there is support out there to feed your baby in the way that best fit both your life and hers.

Engorgement

Engorgement at the outset of nursing is pretty common and can be revisited at any time. One of the foremost organizations in breastfeeding support is La Leche International, which offers a treasure trove of resources for managing nursing issues. Many of the interventions discussed in this chapter are those offered on their website, www.llli.org.

- **Keep your baby with you often.** Holding your baby or allowing them to frequently rest on you can help ease some of the discomfort. That being said, I urge you to take good care of yourself. If it feels too painful to hold your baby, consider trying some other interventions and then returning to this practice.

- **Nurse often.** This may not sound like the most appealing idea, but nursing takes pressure off your boobs. Nursing our baby frequently cultivates the "mother-baby dyad." Lactation consultants refer to this connection as a type of conversation between you, your body, and your baby. You're getting to know each other. The best method for getting to know anyone? Hanging out as often as possible.

- **Hand express.** Easing out even some milk can be helpful. Diane Wiessinger and Teresa Pitman's *The Womanly Art of Breastfeeding* advises to express as follows:
  - Hold your breast with your fingers and thumb cupped around your breast in a C shape.
  - Press your fingers and thumb back toward your chest.
  - Compress your breast between your fingers and thumb, moving them slightly toward your nipple.
  - Release without moving your hand from your breast.
  - Move your hand to a different place around your breast every few compressions or when milk no longer flows.
  - Aim for a spray from one of your nipple pores.
  - Expect this to take up to thirty minutes.
  - This process should *not* feel uncomfortable.
- **Hook up that pump.** If hand expression feels too uncomfortable or is not your jam, a pump can be a godsend. Don't pump until empty. Just pump enough to take the edge off or so your little one can latch.
- **Grab some frozen peas.** Many moms find gel packs or other forms of cooling to be incredibly helpful.

But what about the cabbage leaves? If you never heard about this trick, many moms swear by putting cabbage leaves in their bra or next to their breasts when they feel engorged. While I never used cabbage for this purpose, some women love this method, stating that as the leaves wilt, their engorgement eases. So, once I had a lactation consultant on the phone, I had to ask, "Dianne, what the heck do cabbage leaves have to do with engorgement?"

She laughed. "I am an evidence-based practitioner and feel really strongly about that. There isn't a whole lot of evidence to support the use of cabbage leaves. Researchers have compared cabbage leaves, ice packs, gel packs, and many other remedies for engorgement, without much difference. I personally think, if you use it and swear by it, then good for you. But if it's not evidence based, why not just put an ice pack there instead?"

Blocked Ducts

Another reason moms worry about engorgement is it can lead to blocked ducts. Beyond engorgement, here are a few more culprits behind blocked ducts:

- An interruption in your breastfeeding schedule
- Skipped feeding due to the baby sleeping through a nursing session
- Separation from the baby that results in a skipped feeding or pump session
- Baby on a nursing strike
- Pinchy underwire bras or bras that are too tight

Whatever the reason they develop, most important is recognizing them.

Symptoms of a blocked duct:

- A small lump about the size of a pea or marble
- A fussy baby who isn't getting her normal flow of milk
- Tender area of your breast (but not the whole breast)

"Ugh, I've got a blocked duct—what do I do now?"

- Try nursing often on the affected breast
- Massage the area gently, especially as your baby feeds
- Get in the shower or do something to apply moist heat
- Massage the area in the shower or soak your breast either in a bath or basin
- Hook yourself up to your pump and hand express until your breast softens
- Apply moist heat to your breast before feeding
- Use cold or cooling packs after nursing
- Avoid underwires and wear loose clothing

- Rest. Rest. Rest.
- Reach out for help—a lactation consultant can help with different creative nursing positions to help clear the duct
- Get your shake on (La Leche Interntational recommends a "more unusual treatment is to hold the flat end of an electric toothbrush against [the] blocked duct, and use the vibrations to clear it." If you don't have an electric toothbrush, perhaps a vibrator is worth a try. If you have neither an electric toothbrush nor vibrator, perhaps an early birthday gift is in order—either one results in a brighter smile.)

What's the big deal about blocked ducts? While blocked ducts are not exactly an emergency or an unreasonable amount of discomfort, take them seriously. Clogged ducts can be the road to mastitis. That road sucks. Pun intended.

Blebs

A bleb is like a nipple zit. Just like the ones you get on your face, some blebs hurt and others don't. They look like a little white spot blocking a nipple pore. According to *The Womanly Art of Breastfeeding*, blebs can begin as "a bit of skin over the nipple pore" or a block from higher up in your breast.

Getting rid of blebs (as recommended in *The Womanly Art of Breastfeeding*):
- If it is not bothering you, leave it alone
- Soak it or apply moist heat
- Ask your doctor to resolve it (which will probably involve a small needle)
- Place a cotton ball soaked with vinegar in your bra against the affected area to dissolve the blockage (vinegar dissolves calcium deposits)

Mastitis

As I mentioned at the beginning of this chapter, it was watching my sister fight through three cases of mastitis that taught me how hard nursing could be. My older sister is one tough chick. When I was a kid (and let's be real, still) the sun rose and set on my big sister. Once when she was twelve years old, she fractured her knee ice skating at a pond near our house. When most children would have wailed loud enough to bring ambulances, my sister RODE HER BIKE HOME. Like I said, this is one tough cookie we are talking about. I never heard of mastitis before my sister got it. Bent over, tearful with pain, feverish, her infected breasts landed her in the ER. Mastitis is no joke.

Symptoms of mastitis:
- Red patches or streaks on your breast
- Warm or swollen part of your breast
- Feeling achy, flu-ish, or run-down
- Low-grade fever

"Oh, no—I think I've got it! What now?"
- Call your doctor. Don't wait. Consult about whether you need an antibiotic and how to manage pain
- Keep nursing or pumping frequently, especially on that side
- Keep hydrated
- Rest. Rest. Rest.

Sore Nipples

This is the side effect new moms plan to encounter throughout breastfeeding. Before I became a mother, I could not conceive how nursing would ever be comfortable. Sore nipples happen for a myriad of reasons. Nursing a baby with a tongue tie, moms with flat or inverted nipples, or improperly de-latching your little one can all cause battle-fatigued nipples.

Tips for soothing sore nipples:

- Call a lactation consultant for help with positioning, latching, or de-latching (even if you think your nugget is latched correctly).
- Use lanolin approved for breast care and breastfeeding such as Lansinoh.
- Ask your doctor or midwife for an APNO (all-purpose nipple ointment) prescription
- Brush some of your own milk on your nipples after you are done nursing or pumping

Yeast Infections

If you have been walking around with a vagina for much of your life, you may be used to vigilance for the trademark itching or burning of a yeast infection. Take those symptoms and move them to your breasts and you have the symptoms of a breast yeast infection. Other symptoms include:

- Pink, shiny nipples
- Shooting or stabbing pains in your breasts
- Flaking skin on your nipples
- Yeast is also known as thrush—check your baby's mouth for white areas (moms and babies can pass infections to one another)
- Call your doctor if you suspect a yeast infection. If you notice white areas in your baby's mouth, call your pediatrician.

Your Lactating Body: A Care Manual

All bodies need care, but a lactating, milk-producing, baby-feeding body needs lots of care. When I asked Dianne Cassidy about self-care from her perspective as a lactation consultant, she urged moms, "Take self-care seriously. Showers are not self-care—that is a basic human need. We cannot say 'I had a shower today' and have that suffice. Moms can have a hard time prioritizing themselves. We need to get past this and find a village to help us do that.

Carving out time for you is really important. It can look as simple as reading a book once a day, or going for a cup of coffee on your own. Do not feel guilty about doing this. We put so much of ourselves into these babies and we need to rejuvenate."

Each element offered in this section is a basic need. They are minimums of body maintenance. At the same time, many of us still make excuses for not maintaining even this level of attention to our personal needs. Rest, hydration, and nourishment are foundations for taking care of your amazing, baby-feeding body.

Rest

Nursing and pumping represent opportunities that we rarely take outside of a yoga class or meditation app to slow down for a moment. Especially in the early weeks of feeding, Dianne reminds us of the necessity of taking a pause in the chaos alongside nursing. "Moms need to relax as much as possible and let others do for them. We need to go home, put our feet up, hang out with our baby, and nurse without focusing on all our worries. *Is the baby nursing too much or not enough? Why are they feeding again? Are they getting enough milk? Am I doing this right? Should I get up and pump? We're going to have company, maybe I should cook dinner. I need to do some laundry.* You should be relaxing, feeding your baby, and becoming that mother-baby dyad," Dianne urges. This practice pays dividends throughout the postpartum year.

Hydration

The importance of drinking water while breastfeeding is no secret. Dehydration is a frequent culprit for a milk supply drop. There is no need to make yourself crazy over exacting amounts. Keep water bottles stocked in every location—the diaper bag, feeding nests, your car, office, etc. Drink when you nurse. Have people fill bottles for your nursing nest. Pay attention to your body signals. When water tastes ultra-refreshing, you probably need to drink a bunch more of it. Breastfeeding dries you out.

While important for water consumption, equally vital is moisturizing. This was another surprise intervention pelvic floor specialist, Kathy Kates, NP, brought up in our interview on pelvic floor health. "Dryness contributes to muscle tightness," Kathy explains. "It also exacerbates existing tightness and weakness in the pelvic floor. Think about how tight your skin feels in the winter if you don't use moisturizing cream. People are not used to feeling their pelvic floor, so they have no idea how dry they are until they feel moisturized. In addition to internal moisturization, also moisturize the vulva and labia externally." Kathy recommends natural, plant-based moisturizers designed for caring for your vulva and vagina (search Amazon.com for vaginal moisturizers). When returning to sex and throughout your entire breastfeeding tenure, your vagina and vulva will lack natural lubrication. Pair moisturization with regular routines, such as showering.

Kathy says, "When you're breastfeeding, estrogen levels drop and the vagina gets super dry. It needs estrogen to plump it up." This is further discussed in Chapter 11 (page 193) on sex as well. "Changes happen to the lining of your vaginal wall—the mucosa. When working with a postpartum mom having pain with sex (that she never experienced before having a baby), the first thing I inquire about is what she does to lubricate the vaginal walls. Women often claim they don't need additional lubrication. I urge them to try consistent lubrication for a week and then check in. Inevitably, people come back saying how much better they feel." The incorporation of lube in sex is not just for comfort but also the health of your pelvic floor.

Movement

Nursing can be difficult to balance with time for movement. Breastfeeding requires stillness and sitting so much of the time. While many of us crave a leap back into exercise, proceed carefully. The hormones of breastfeeding keep chemicals such as relaxin present in your body, resulting in potential risk of overstretching or injury. These chemicals make us more flexible than we expect. For those of us who spend our lives with short hamstrings and a tight back, this may feel like a miracle. If you are excited about movement and have been cleared to engage in it, go for it. However, consider spending extra time on stability work to help prevent injury. Consult Chapter 8 on page 135 for guidance on reintroducing exercise.

Feed the Milk Factory

"I want oatmeal," I said after hearing my husband read the breakfast choices.

"Really? Did you hear that I said pancakes?" he questioned, never having seen me order oatmeal for breakfast in the course of our relationship. Certainly not when pancakes, eggs, waffles, or even granola was on the menu.

"Oatmeal," I say, looking at the minutes-old baby on my chest.

I realize oatmeal from a hospital cafeteria sounds like some sort of punishment, but I promise you, it was the best bowl of oatmeal of my entire life. It was clearly exactly what my body needed, when I needed it. Hence, one of my favorite go-to breakfasts was born.

It takes food to make food. Some moms are surprised to find themselves even hungrier while nursing than when they were pregnant. This is why we must prioritize meals and keep snacks in our nursing nest. Sometimes nursing or pumping are the few times when we have a second to feed ourselves.

But what *should* I be eating? There is rarely better click-bait for a new mom than "The top foods you must eat while you are nursing" or "Eat this to increase your milk supply." As moms, we want to know the best answers, to do right by these little creatures we adore. It becomes so easy to get sucked down the rabbit hole trying to eat the perfect foods for your baby. On one side, the eating disorder therapist in me bristles at the concept of eating just the right foods to produce a desired effect. The attempt to control our bodies with food is treacherous ground. On the other side of things, I would have bet my breast pump that oatmeal helped me produce milk.

This is why I was so excited to connect with lactation consultants with such rigorous, evidence-based standards on the *Momma Bites!* podcast. When I spoke with Alia Macrina, IBCLC, I asked her about lactogenic (milk-producing) foods. "The evidence-based research for it is minimal," she explains. "If eating something safe helps a mom feel like she's doing something, then that may help." In psychology, we call this principle self-efficacy—the idea that taking any step to help ourselves generally makes us feel better. "As an IBCLC who sees moms who struggle with low milk supply, I'm never going to undercut the science that we do know—which is to keep moving the milk. Taking milk out makes more milk, end of story. Nothing is ever going to replace a well-latched baby on the breast. This is the most effective way keep your supply up."

Stop making yourself crazy trying to figure out how to consume oatmeal, nuts, avocados, and fennel seeds every day. Honor your body with gentle nutrition and hydration. Balance foods in the way you would intuitively, without exclusion or obsession (consult Chapter 5, "Feeding Yourself" (page 89), for more information about this). Think about what you might want at the ready in your kitchen and have it stocked up. This is a practical and easy way for people to help out. Keep foods around that you can eat with one hand: sandwiches, finger foods, something that can be easily speared with a fork or picked up with a spoon. And don't freak about every single micronutrient. Your provider will probably keep you on prenatal vitamins throughout your course of nursing anyway.

Foods to avoid while breastfeeding:
- Poison

I'm kidding. But many moms get completely obsessed with consuming the "right" foods at this time. Here is La Leche International's stance on food choice:

> There are no foods you need to avoid while breastfeeding. Some strongly flavored foods may change the taste of your milk, but many babies seem to enjoy a variety of breast milk flavors! Often

the dominant flavors of your diet—whether soy sauce, chili, garlic, or something else—were in your amniotic fluid during pregnancy. Before birth, babies swallow amniotic fluid and are accustomed to these flavors before tasting them in your milk.

In the postpartum year, life can feel a little crazy. The baby sleeps or does not sleep whenever she wants. Sometimes he cluster-feeds, other times it feels like your boobs will explode when he takes a long nap. In these situations, it can feel like what we put into our bodies is the one place we have control. We will even blame ourselves for things out of our power ("he's been up all night—I shouldn't have had chocolate"). This gives us the illusion of control. Despite the accompanying self-blame, we take it as long as it comes with the (albeit inaccurate) belief that we can change these outcomes through our own behavior.

Food Allergies and Restrictions

"I'm concerned about my wife," Chloe tells me in session four months after her baby's arrival. Chloe and I have been working together for four years. With hard work and therapy, she eliminated her eating disorder related behaviors and remains consistent in her recovery-oriented attitude. Like many people who struggle with addictions or eating disorders, she is also skillful at noticing eating disorder–related behaviors in others.

"What's going on?"

"It's Wyatt. He's so fussy. She's worried he could have a food allergy or sensitivity. Everything she reads and even the pediatrician told her to try eliminating some of the common allergens from her diet while nursing. First it started with dairy. Pretty quickly she seemed obsessed. She'd freak out if a dairy product was cooked into something she ate. Between the restriction, no longer being pregnant, and all the nursing, she's losing a lot of weight at once. People keep giving her all these compliments. Now, she's wondering if he could be allergic to nuts, or maybe even soy. I know it's for totally different reasons, but the elimination and obsession reminds me of myself when my eating disorder started."

"Have you shared this with her?"

"I tried a little. She wasn't really open to hearing it. She says she feels like she has to do *something*. I get it. He gets really fussy and nothing works. I can see she feels like she's taking steps by eliminating foods, but it doesn't seem clear that it's helping him."

As a therapist who specializes in treating eating disorders, I have a particular perspective on moms' concerns around food allergies in their babies. With each challenge their baby presents, I see the moms in my practice (even those without eating disorders) scrutinize every last food they eat. "The baby seems fussy—is it because of what I ate today?" "He won't sleep—is that because there's not enough protein in my breastmilk?" "Is this colic or a food allergy?" The questions go on and on. Since the evidence is not always clear, many of us are left wondering if a food allergy can explain our child's difficult symptoms. This is also our culture's favorite solution—food allergy or sensitivities. These instances tempt moms onto elimination diets to determine if there is an issue. For example, many nursing moms with colicky babies experiment with food eliminations, hoping to stop the crying. Who could blame them? However, this is one of the most vulnerable times of our lives. Sometimes when we reach for food as the explanation, we are actually seeking that control. While control sounds like a good thing here, at the same time, the last thing you need to add to your list of tasks is combing through ingredient labels of every food you consume searching for traces of dairy or soy.

In 2017, a study conducted at the pediatric center in Cheil General Hospital & Women's Healthcare Center in Korea reported that over a third of the 145 participants who self-imposed food restrictions while breastfeeding experienced significant discomfort with these restrictions. There was no medical reason reported for these restrictions. The field of maternal research needs to do more studies like these. So many of us reach for things to help make sense of or change an experience. Paradoxically, this results in the opposite of self-care. We make things more challenging for ourselves as an attempt to control the things that are outside of us.

According to La Leche International, signs of a food allergy in babies include:

- Vomiting, especially projectile vomiting
- Diarrhea
- Blood in stool
- Poor weight gain
- Presenting as if wanting to nurse and then pulling away or arching
- Rash

If your baby has these symptoms, consult your pediatrician. If you have a history of an eating disorder or disordered eating (chronic dieting, restrained eating, bingeing), I urge you to disclose this to your pediatrician if they plan to prescribe an elimination diet for allergy investigation. Our current medical culture often casually endorses restriction as a means of exploration. This is irresponsible. A significant number of women in my practice developed their eating disorders in adulthood after prescribed food eliminations when providers could not pinpoint causes of digestive distress. Let providers know how triggering food elimination could be for you. If the provider is not understanding (or even worse, shames you), find a new provider. Remember, this is a person who will be treating your child over the course of years—you want them savvy in understanding how eating disorders, recovery, and triggers work. If you attempt an elimination diet and your baby does not change in presentation, make sure to add restricted foods back into your diet before eliminating another class of foods. Sometimes when folks board the restriction train, they continue riding it, adding restriction rather than swapping out eliminated foods.

If you remain on a restriction regimen for the duration of breastfeeding, consider reaching out to a supportive provider, namely an intuitive eating-trained dietitian or therapist who can assist with the task of reintro-ducing restricted foods. Even those without a history of dieting can feel trig-gered toward disordered eating behaviors (e.g., bingeing or food avoidance).

Your Hormones & Emotions: A Care Manual
Worry

"I wish I had a little gauge on my boobs to tell how much milk he's getting," Natasha says, leaning over to pull a piece of lint off her sleeping baby's head, "I'm just so worried that he's not getting enough."

I get it. I had the same fantasy of somehow quantifying my baby's con-sumption when I was nursing. Vague approximations of ounces found on Google searches only made me increasingly frantic to know exactly how much they drank. *If only I knew*, my mind seduced.

Also, Natasha and I predicted this thought pattern prior to her delivery. Struggling with a nasty case of generalized anxiety prior to pregnancy, she worried her way through all nine months of gestation. "Do you remember when you would wish you could have an ultrasound once a day?" I ask, and she cracks a smile.

"I know," she says, chuckling. "I would just find something else to worry about. But still, I wish there was a way to find out…" She trails off, her mind still grasping for a strategy to ascertain an answer to her latest source of anxiety.

We live in a world where we are flooded with information and monitor-ing. Our devices deliver wide approximations of how much we move and sleep. Increasingly, we *feel* like we know more and therefore our tolerance for the unknown shrinks. This is one of the things that makes pregnancy and early parenthood so difficult. We are responsible for the welfare of a new, ever-changing being. Our baby's vulnerability to survival magnifies all of our own emotions. We want to know more. We obsess over the scraps of infor-mation their bodies tell us—pee, poop, the pitch of their cries, sound of their coos, their feeding and sleep patterns. "If I could just quantify it," we tell our-selves, "I could relax a little more."

"Fears about whether babies are getting enough is one of those things that, no matter how much you educate, moms still worry,'" Dianne Cassidy, IBCLC, states. "I remember that even for my kids. We teach moms if the babies are pooping and peeing, they are getting enough. If it's coming in, it's going out. It sounds so simple, but it really is the bottom line. I remember my sister telling me that and feeling, 'That's telling me nothing, I need something better to go on.'" Even Dianne chased the wish for a solid, numeric answer.

Hormones

The hormones of breastfeeding can be a roller coaster. Oxytocin, vasopressin, and prolactin are in a constant dance making breastfeeding possible. Even when nursing goes well, hormone levels fluctuate producing a variety of experiences. Dianne Cassidy further explains. "Breastfeeding is so hormonal. It really affects how you feel. Oxytocin is everybody's favorite hormone in the birth world. This love hormone is so important in childbirth, labor, and feeding the baby. It makes you feel good—connects and bonds you. When you feed your baby, oxytocin surges through your system."

While getting off on our oxytocin high, we also ride the prolactin wave. Prolactin is responsible for milk production, but it also can be the culprit behind the moodiness we feel. When nursing past four to six months, you might feel an extra bump in moodiness at the time milk production naturally drops a bit. Moms may struggle to reach out for help so far in the postpartum year. *I've made it this far, why would I need support now? I feel silly asking for help at this point.* I have heard this argument. At times, in my own head. Cut it out. Struggle at any point is the time to reach out.

Hormonal fluctuations make us more vulnerable to unhelpful mindsets such as overwhelm, depression, and irritability. Adding the various life circumstances of a new mom—going back to work, acclimating a sibling, returning to sex (including reintroduction of birth control in many cases)—and we find ourselves in a hormonal hurricane. If you sense you are dealing with a postpartum mood disorder, consult Chapter 7 on page 117. If you have thoughts or urges to hurt yourself, your baby, or anyone else, that is the time to head to the emergency room. Do not delay.

A Few Really Bad Minutes: Dysphoric Milk Ejection Reflex

I started noticing it when I was pumping at work. Initially I tried to ignore the sadness, brush it off with every possible excuse. But then without fail, a crash of sadness each time I pumped . . . until my milk let down. I consulted every knowledgeable mom and professional I could find.

"It's like someone died," I told them. "I am absolutely destroyed, totally despondent with grief. Then I hear the milk spraying against the flanges and I realize the feeling is gone."

Gone. As abruptly as it arrived.

My inquiries were met with furrowed brows. My savviest providers responded by assessing for postpartum depression.

"No," I'd answer. "I don't think this is PPD. I've had depression. I know what that is like. This is different. It feels hormonal, some sort of weird response to pumping."

No answers.

I nearly forgot about it until it blasted back onto the scene when I had my son. The despondency squashed my motivation to pump. Even though I knew it would go away as soon as my milk let down, it was hard to muster the gumption to strap cold plastic to my overheated boobs and sit in abject sadness. As a result, I could not store enough milk and had to supplement with formula.

When researching this book and revisiting my experiences of nursing and pumping, a rush of memory sent me back to the days where I sat at my desk between sessions and cried my way through the first few minutes of pumping. One more time, I took a crack at the Google machine to find if I was the only crazy lady on the planet who sobbed before the milk started flowing.

Then I found it.

Dysphoric milk ejection reflex.

Within hours I had Alia Macrina, IBLC and researcher, booked on the *Momma Bites!* podcast. Alia was the first to name dysphoric milk ejection reflex or D-MER after experiencing a sudden onset nursing her third child. "I had severe despondent D-MER. It was a significant, negative, emotional experience when I had it. It really helped that I worked in lactation because once I connected it to letdown, I realized it can't just be me."

Moms with D-MER report a myriad of experiences—sadness, anxiety, despondency, suicidality, rage, and nausea. On her site, Alia defines D-MER as "a condition affecting lactating women characterized by an abrupt dysphoria, or negative emotions, that occur just before milk release and continuing not more than a few minutes." While D-MER is in many lactation textbooks, it is not in the *Diagnostics & Standards Manual* (the manual that defines many of the most common psychiatric disorders) so it's not even something our providers know a lot about, Alia explains. She told me about thousands of women dealing with D-MER who reached out to her. "'There is a significant number of women that come to me who cannot even tell their partner. They feel comfort and camaraderie on the message boards but shame about disclosing to others who might not understand." Not only do women dealing with D-MER feel an intense "sense of personal shame about the condition, but this is intensified by the fact that the disorder can manifest as shame. This experience is so counter to the 'breast is best,' Madonna-esque image the pro-breastfeeding movement portrays which does a disservice to women who struggle."

"D-MER changes as your baby ages. In a lot of cases, the body will self-correct as the baby grows. A lot of moms with mild D-MER find after three to six months, it lifts. A lot of moms with moderate D-MER find between nine and twelve months, it starts to lift. Severe D-MER can last past the first year. It seems as the milk supply changes and the baby grows, hormones of lactation do start changing. Whatever way these changes happen, some moms find relief."

Treating D-MER

For moms dealing with D-MER, Alia reports that education is key. In fact, education is the main treatment. "The most powerful 'treatment' is knowing the feeling is real but not true. That is why many moms find distraction to be most helpful. A woman with D-MER is having an emotional experience that is not valid. It's real, but not valid—so you don't have to turn your attention toward it. You don't need to be curious about it, you don't need to be aware of it. You need to turn on the latest episode of *Orange Is the New Black* and pretend it's not happening."

If you are dealing with D-MER, reach out for help. Consult Alia's website and join her Facebook group, both listed in the Resources section on page 229. Connect with others who understand your pain. If you consult with a therapist, inquire whether they know about this condition or have any interest in learning about it.

Taking the Breastfeeding Show on the Road: How to Nurse in Public

The parking lot of Petco. The café area of Target. The veterinarian's office during our beloved cat's euthanizing, ending his battle with cancer. You name it, I nursed there. Here are some favorite stories that moms shared with me about the unexpected places they had to nurse or pump:

- "Pumping in the car, while driving! Also, once I had the pump hanging off my boob in the office, a colleague opened the door, and my clients' parents were right there. Oops."
- "Inside Howard Hughes' plane, The Spruce Goose. It is at an aviation museum nearby and we went for a Father's Day."
- "At the X-Games with motorcycles jumping and standing room only."
- "At a tattoo parlor while my friends got tattoos honoring my deceased friend."
- "Walking from our parking spot at Sounders games. Now I pump for my second in the drive-through for Starbucks."

- "On an airplane while waiting for the plane to de-ice. This was before 'hooter hiders' so my fellow travelers got a good view."

Maybe you're nursing this kid like a boss. Or maybe you still feel like a mess, but if you sit on your couch any longer, you are going to lose it. Whatever the reason, momma needs to leave the house. Isolation is a true problem for moms of newborns. While going out can feel overwhelming at times, it is important for your mental and physical health. In venturing out, you face the challenge of feeding your baby in public. Some women have little issue with nursing in public. For others, managing modesty is an issue in itself. If privacy is a stumbling block, start venturing out places where you can excuse yourself to nurse in private—dressing rooms, your car, or nursing lounges.

Explore nursing with a coverup, a modest shirt, or just slide the strap of that tank top down and feed your baby. The choices around breastfeeding are personal and there are no wrong answers. Your level of modesty need only be consistent with your values. It is legal to breastfeed in all fifty states; however, each state has its own individual laws. For more information on your rights in breastfeeding and pumping, consult the Resources section on page 229. There are a variety of communities, including the Facebook group associated with *The Badass Breastfeeder Podcast* to support moms breastfeeding in public without apology.

If you struggle to get rolling with breastfeeding wherever you want to, think of this as a self-care issue. No matter your breastfeeding goals, it is not a viable solution to stay trapped in your house. Nursing in public is an exercise in allowing yourself to take up space, prioritizing yourself and your baby. This can be a challenge for women. From a young age, we receive messages telling us to take up less space, whether in body size, obedience, or getting along. If others have a problem with your nursing, let it be their issue rather than yours.

Pumping

"FFFFFFt . . . ffffft . . . fffffft . . . ping!" the whir of my pump is interrupted by an alert from my phone.

Rachel: [picture of two full bottles of milk]

Me: Woah. You must be feeling a lot better.

Rachel: Can't lie. I'm pretty proud of this. But I woke up with boulders for boobs.

Me: [Laughing emoji] It's pretty impressive.

Rachel: I was just reading something yesterday that cows only pump once a day for milk. Those bitches have no idea how good they've got it.

Ah, pumping. The simultaneous lifeline and bane of many postpartum moms' existence. Knowing when and how to incorporate pumping can feel like trying to jump into a game of double-dutch when you can barely skip rope. As days of maternity leave turn to weeks, clients often arrive to session caught in an anxiety loop. *When do I start pumping? What if I pump and then he wakes up? He won't have enough milk. What if I do all this work and she won't drink expressed milk? What if he hates the frozen milk?*

"If moms and babies are feeding fine in those first two weeks of life, I always tell moms 'don't pump.'" Dianne Cassidy informed me. "If they're feeding fine, you're feeling good, you're not having trouble, you're not separated from each other, there's no issues, don't worry about pumping for the first few weeks. Let your body adjust to the baby's needs before we introduce anything else. Your body works on supply and demand—your body makes the milk, and baby is taking it. If you nurse your baby every couple of hours all day long and also try to pump in those first two weeks of life, that encourages way more milk than you need."

What do we do if we need to be away from our babies or introduce a breast-milk bottle? In these cases, Dianne advises, "Work with a lactation consultant to help balance what is too much or too little. Any time after the first couple of weeks is fine to start pumping whenever you want. Moms worry there's not going to be any milk for the baby. But that's not the case. Your breasts are constantly making milk. They're never empty. And the pump doesn't take all the milk—there's always some left in the breast. Again, your body works on supply and demand, so if you pump and then feed the baby, you're really just telling your body to make more milk. It's this perfect system we constantly doubt."

Pumping can be a major issue in the life of a postpartum mom. Breastfeeding is challenging enough without having to remember whether we packed the teeny tiny white valve things that make the pump work but are inconveniently the size of a fingertip. If you need a breast pump, contact your insurance provider. According to healthcare.gov, "Your health insurance plan must cover the cost of a breast pump. It may be either a rental unit or a new one you'll keep. Your plan may have guidelines on whether the covered pump is manual or electric, the length of the rental, and when you'll receive it (before or after birth)." Getting a prescription from your doctor for a pump can be helpful coverage for pump cost (also called pre authorization). If you have a health spending account, you can quickly purchase a pump and related supplies. While money is tight for many families dealing with maternity leave, a second pump and equipment can be an absolute miracle for a commuting mother.

A well-packed pump bag includes:
- All the pumping equipment
    - Bottles to pump into
    - Flanges
    - Membranes (extra of these, they escape when you least expect it)
    - Valves
    - Tubing
    - Hands-free expression bra (in a pinch, a sports bra with strategically cut holes works too)
    - Breastmilk storage bags

- Cooler bag and ice pack to transport milk
- Sharpie for labeling bags
- The plug and/or batteries
- Item of your baby's to snuggle or picture to look at, even if just on your phone, which can help your milk let down
- Coverup, if that's your jam
- Mode of entertainment (phone, magazine, the legal brief you're racing to finish)
- Extra breast pads
- Sign to keep out peeps who don't want to get flashed by a milk-pumping mom
- Extra shirt

If you are in transit with your pump, chances are you are pumping at work. Here are the absolute basic coverages for pumping at work according to the United States Department of Labor:

Federal employees and hourly employees in the private sector are entitled to a "reasonable break time . . . to express breast milk for her nursing child for one year after the child's birth each time such employee has the need to express the milk." The law continues, "Employers are also required to provide 'a place other than a bathroom, that is shielded from view and free from intrusion from coworkers and the public, which may be used by an employee to express breast milk" (Affordable Care Act, Fair Labor Standards Act as quoted in Shortall 2015, 59).

Sounds pretty sweet, right? Here are the catches as explained in Jessica Shortall's book *Work. Pump. Repeat.* (Required reading for pumping mothers!) The law contains vague language like "reasonable break time" and "a place other than a bathroom," which can make it tough to pin down the exact protections of the laws. One person's "reasonable" amount of time to pump might only get another mom halfway there. Shortall also reminds us that "non-bathroom space doesn't have to be permanent; it can be temporary or made available when needed" (Shortall 2015, 58).

Prepping for pumping at work:
- Google. The laws discussed above are federal and may not apply to the private sector.
- Investigate the laws in your state governing pumping in the workplace. They differ by state.
- Check out your employee handbook.
- Chat with the other moms in your office. What was their experience of nursing? These ladies will be the most important sources of information in this journey. They know the spots for pumping, milk storage, and who to talk to in HR to help support this effort.

Weaning

The last day I ever nursed was supposed to be the fourth of July. I had not intended it to be, but that was just how things went. My son showed many of the signs that he was done. He ate table foods well. Easily distracted, he de-latched several times during his feedings. Despite all of the parenting advice, he often fell asleep during his afternoon feed. This day, he fell into a nap without nursing. After his nap came snack, dinner, and soon bedtime. This seemed like the day to stop.

I felt a mix of sadness and freedom moving on to his next step. Acutely aware he is my last baby, that would be my last ever feeding. Titrating slowly to this point, my left breast easily got the message. It returned to its pre-baby form. My right breast (his preferred side) struggled. It felt a bit full, but nothing compared to the engorgement I experienced over my nursing tenure. I waited for it to return to its previous shape. But it didn't. Over the next several days, my breasts seemed to be settling into vastly different identities. Despite over a week without a latched baby, the right one still felt ready to nurse. Ten days later I could not take it any longer. Simultaneously worried I would set back ten days of forward movement, but also fearing mastitis, I decided to nurse him one last time. Again, he nursed, cozy and warm in a cross-cradle hold. This time I cried, mourning the loss of nursing, feeling this milestone in our relationship. We were ready to be done and yet I still felt the loss. He fell asleep while nursing and I snuggled him, soothed by the sound of his breathing. My right breast instantly returned to its pre-baby shape. I tucked it back into my shirt, grateful for my body's wisdom knowing we all needed just one last time.

While weaning, Dianne urges moms to remember, "It can't be done overnight. Deciding when you want to wean is very different than letting your baby wean on their own. Keep in mind that it is about both of you. This is the only thing your baby has ever known since day one of his life. This is a huge change in connection, so we need to foster lots of care and love through this process."

How to begin weaning:

- Set your expectations accordingly. This is going to take a while. The ramp-up for breastfeeding is a rapid climb; think of weaning as a slow descent.
- Watch your baby and your body for easiest-to-drop feedings and then take a little bit of the feed away at a time.
- As difficult as it might be, try to make yourself unavailable around the feeding time you try to drop, as your baby may want to feed if you're there. ("Geez, I wasn't wanting pizza for dinner, but now that I walked past my favorite pizza place, I really want pizza!")
- To prevent engorgement and discomfort, La Leche recommends expressing milk as needed. This does not have to be an entire pumping session, but rather just to keep you comfortable.
- Make sure to replace bonding time. This is for your baby but also you. Weaning can be a difficult transition.

Weaning self-care:

- "Some of those hormonal changes can be serious. We have to make sure we're not just cutting it off," Dianne Cassidy advises. "Make sure your body has time to adapt to the changes that happen by taking a little bit of the feeds away a little at a time. It's a process for sure."

- Request hugs or compassionate touch from those around you. Schedule a massage.

- Be on the lookout for weaning depression. If you have been keeping your eyes peeled for postpartum mood disorders, add this one to the list. Little is known about causes of weaning depression. It is suspected that the drop in oxytocin results in an experience of depression. Do not wait to seek support. Even if you think this is "just" weaning depression, reach out to your medical and psychological providers if you notice yourself beginning to struggle.

Notes

Cassidy, Dianne. "Dianne Cassidy, IBCLC, on Breastfeeding and Badassery." Interviewed by Corinne Crossley, *Momma Bites! podcast*, October 3, 2019.

Centers for Disease Control and Prevention. "Rates of Breastfeeding Continue to Rise" Last accessed September 25, 2019. https://www.cdc.gov/media/releases/2016/p0822-breastfeeding-rates.html

La Leche League International. "Guide to Breastfeeding." Accessed November 15, 2019. https://www.llli.org/breastfeeding-info/

Macrina, Alia. "What a Letdown! Dysphoric Milk Ejection Reflex." Interview by Corinne Crossley, *Momma Bites! podcast*, September 11, 2019.

Medela. "Reasons for Blocked Ducts." Last accessed October 15. 2019. https://www.medela.com/breastfeeding-professionals/education/lactation-period/blocked-ducts

Medela. "Postpartum Hormones and How They Affect You." Last accessed December 26, 2019. http://www.medelabreastfeedingus.com/article/172/postpartum-hormonal-changes-&-how-they-affect-you

National Conference of State Legislatures. "Breastfeeding State Laws." Last accessed November 29, 2019. http://www.ncsl.org/research/health /breastfeeding-state-laws.aspx

Pearson, Catherine., "Weaning and Depression Linked in Many Women." Huffington Post, February 27, 2012. https://www.huffpost.com/entry /weaning-depression-link-breastfeeding-postpartum-depression_n _1301233

Shortall, Jessica. *Work. Pump. Repeat.* New York: Abrams, 2015.

Wiessinger, Diane, Diane West, and Teresa Pitman. La Leche League. *The Womanly Art of Breastfeeding* New York: Balantine, 2010.

Chapter 5:
A Mom's Gotta Eat
Feeding Yourself

I am sitting in a booth across from my friend Rachel and her baby. In front of me is a sandwich; beside me, my baby sleeps. In front of Rachel is a delicious-looking salad, untouched. Her baby wails as she assembles a bottle with the stealth of a pit crew. The breastmilk bag sits in warm water, slowly heating. Her daughter's cries get louder.

"Screw this, I'm just going to give it to her cold," she says, pouring the milk into the bottle with lightning precision. She scoops her daughter out of the car seat and presents the bottle.

Silence.

Rachel exhales and sits back against the booth. I see her glance at her dish and then look away. My best friend pumps breastmilk every four hours around the clock, so I know she is famished, even if she is unable to eat without a free hand.

I pick up her fork and begin spearing food from her plate. "I know this might seem a little weird, but can I help you?" I ask, offering the fork to her.

She takes a bite. "Thank you. You don't have to do this."

"I know. But you'd do the same for me and I don't want to sit here eating in front of you knowing that you must be starving."

I gather more food onto the fork and offer it again.

Motherhood completely changes the way we feed ourselves. With every other need for the baby prioritized above our own, we put off eating until we fall into scavenging. We eat on the go, subsist on grabbed snacks, and feel out of control when we find ourselves over-hungry. Given these routines in early motherhood, it is effortless to slip into making meals of leftover toddler food or surviving on the box of raisins at the bottom of the diaper bag.

There are many reasons why we deprioritize feeding our bodies. Exhaustion renders us out of touch with our bodies. Some moms feel unable to sit down to a meal if their baby cries for them. In high-needs phases, this results in days without a real meal. And let's not forget about all the ways we may slide into a restriction mindset with the hope of weight loss at the back of our minds. Some moms use the constant on-the-go nature of postpartum life to justify their passive restriction.

Here's the deal: you need to eat. All moms need to eat. If you are nursing, you need fuel to make milk. If you're not nursing, you need fuel to keep functioning. Postpartum moms are already depleted, the last thing you need is to be undernourished. How do you know whether you need to eat? In most cases—hunger. How do you know when you have had enough? You get full.

Intuitive Eating

Following your own hunger, satiety, and body signals is called intuitive eating. Prior to 1995, Evelyn Tribole, RD, and Elyse Resch, RD, both had thriving nutrition practices with clients they adored. There was just one problem. The clients given weight-loss plans failed miserably. It was not for a lack of trying on the part of clinician or client. If they sought to truly help, Resch and Tribole knew they had to reevaluate their directives (and the directives of the nutrition community). After much study, they published *Intuitive Eating*.

Intuitive eating entails listening to your body and following its cues. Centered on ten principals, this approach honors hunger, fullness, and satisfaction, rejects diet mentality, and includes caring for our whole body respectfully (by exercising, etc.). "Intuitive eating is not an absolute plan, but guidelines to help you have more satisfaction and feel better," Elyse explained when we chatted on the *Momma Bites!* podcast. "There's no perfection—nothing about intuitive eating has anything to do with perfection."

Let's get the ball rolling with a bit of awareness around hunger and satiety signals.

Exercise: Your Hunger Scale

Feel free to try this exercise over the course of several hours. Take some time to think. How do you know when you're hungry? There are many different levels of hunger:

Famished: Lightheaded, hangry, experiencing headaches, irritability, fuzzy thinking

Very Hungry: Focused on getting food, ready to eat immediately, irritable if forced to wait for food, stomach growling

Hungry: Excited to eat, can wait a little longer if required, mouth waters easily, food tastes great when eating, stomach feels ready for food but not painfully empty

Peckish: Characterized by the sentiment "I could eat" but food does not feel required, easily able to wait if necessary, highly palatable foods are most appealing while other foods are less interesting

Satisfied: Awareness that body is adequately fed, if interrupted could easily move on, food begins to taste a little less delicious compared to initial bites, stomach no longer empty or signaling for more

Full: Feeling of fullness in stomach, food less appealing, post-meal movement less comfortable

Overfull: Stomach uncomfortable, bloated, or distended, feeling overly warm in body, heartburn or reflux symptoms of food repeating, difficulty moving or sleeping

Now, consider the ways that you know you are hungry at each of these levels. Write signs of each level of hunger you notice in your body:

Famished:

_____

_____

_____

_____

_____

Hungry:

_____

_____

_____

_____

_____

Peckish:

_____

_____

_____

_____

How do you know when you're full or getting full? What happens when you are overfull? What are some of the signs *inside your body* that you are ready to stop eating? What does it feel like when you are full?

Satisfied/getting full:

_____

_____

_____

_____

_____

Full:

_____

_____

_____

_____

_____

Overfull/stuffed:

_____

_____

_____

_____

What does it feel like in your body when you are neither hungry nor full? Does that have a physical or mental experience? Note it here.

_____

_____

_____

_____

_____

Review your answers from the exercise thus far. Plot the cues you defined for each level of hunger, satisfaction, and fullness along this line.

←───────────────────────────────────────→

Famished   **Stuffed**

This is your personal hunger scale. Woohoo! Way to go! This hunger scale represents physical experiences you sense in your body. Throughout your postpartum year, your hunger and satiety scale will likely evolve and change. The more we can tune into our bodies as a source of information, the more powerful we become in understanding our own needs. These signals are the bedrock of mindful and intuitive eating. No one else can tell you what they are, only your body.

These signals are simply something to notice. No one follows them perfectly. "There are ways of intuitive eating that don't have to be so complicated," Elyse says. "People are scared it means they have to rate every bite of food with a number on the hunger scale. It's nothing like that. It's more about paying attention to how you feel." Use these signals to go forth and be curious. See what works for your body and does not.

What to Eat?

Now you know where you are on the hunger scale. But, what to eat? Focusing so much on our kids' needs and the "right" foods leaves us struggling to know what we want. We force ourselves to exist on what's available, without any planning or regard to our own needs.

To figure out what we want to eat, we have to listen to our bodies. My clients balk at this idea. "I don't have time for that! I can't sit there all day in meditation, searching my soul for what I want for lunch!" For those who spend stretches of time in diet or restriction mentality, ascertaining what they want feels overwhelming and time consuming. If this is where you are, I promise with practice it gets easier. Soon this method will be light-years faster than externally based (diet) messages. Refer back to your hunger scale. This information is the foundation of this decision.

Exercise: What to Eat?

Do this exercise in advance of being hungry. When hungry, we have trouble thinking outside the box, especially if we're busy with our babies.

On a separate piece of paper, make a list of foods that match each level of hunger from your hunger scale. If you're having trouble thinking of choices, some are listed below. When it's time to eat, check in with your hunger scale above and choose from the list of foods to enjoy that match each level of hunger:

Famished
- Bowl of oatmeal with banana and walnuts
- Omelet, toast, and fruit
- Avocado toast with bacon and egg
- Bagel with cream cheese or peanut butter
- Sandwich with significant amount of protein
- Soup and sandwich
- Salad topped with chicken, side of bread
- Pasta with protein (chicken parm, meatballs)
- Quinoa bowl with added protein (chicken or egg)
- Chili with cornbread

Very Hungry
- Fish tacos
- Salmon, broccoli, sweet potato
- Hearty soup with bread
- Sandwich with veggies and hummus

- Breakfast sandwich with fruit
- Grain bowl with vegetables
- Mac and cheese with broccoli
- Ice cream sundae
- Full fat yogurt with lots of granola

Hungry

- Greek yogurt with mix-ins
- Apple and peanut butter
- Bagel with cream cheese
- Cottage cheese with fruit
- Veggies, dip, cheese
- Cereal
- Hardboiled egg and some berries
- Chicken tenders and veggies or fruit
- Sushi
- Bowl of ice cream
- Nachos with guacamole and protein

Peckish

- Smoothie
- Dried fruit
- Berries
- Cheese stick
- Crackers
- Naan or pita and hummus
- Pastry

Neither Hungry nor Full

- Tea
- Water

- Hard candy
- Gum

Satisfied, Full, or Overfull
- Tea (especially mint or ginger)
- Gum

Please see page 233 for some of my favorite recipes.

How to Eat

"I can never pay attention to my food," Amy answers. We are in the process of examining her nightly overeating pattern.

"Why? What's going on?" I ask.

"What do you mean? There's always something. At work, I eat while working. At home, I eat while I make things for the kids. I snack while driving."

"So, you never have a moment to pay attention to what you are eating when you are eating it?"

"That's correct."

"No wonder you binge at night!" I exclaim.

"I don't understand," she looks puzzled.

"You are always running, doing, and caretaking. The only time you take all day to notice what you eat is when you are exhausted, full of a day's worth of stress. This is the first chance for you to notice taste, texture, and satisfaction."

"Wait, that's important?"

Intuitive eating is based on mindfulness. Do not get freaked out! This is not the assignment to sit on a meditation cushion with a single raisin (though that's a good one). Rather, this is just about getting us to notice what we are doing.

Mindful Enough Eating

Mindful eating for mothers probably sounds impossible. "I think of mindful eating as something we do slowly, tasting all the flavors and textures in a bite, so it takes an hour to finish a strawberry. Those versions of mindful eating are valuable," Lindsay Stenovec, RD, host of *The Embodied & Well Mom Show*, defines in our interview. "But really, mindfulness is simply using awareness to pay attention to something without judgment. It's not about outcomes. Being able to drop into our bodies, check in with our thoughts, emotions, and physical sensations throughout the eating process is helpful. It's about noticing taste, texture, smell, and how food physically feels in our bodies. As moms, this looks more like little check-ins. So, if we're sitting with kids at a chaotic family meal that is affecting our eating, mindfulness is doing our best to drop the judgment and be aware of what's going on in that meal. That may inform us on next steps for self-care. I've worked with moms where this elicits an opportunity for compassion. For example, 'The noise that my child is making elicits strong emotions in my body—my throat feels tight, my belly is in knots, and I have a headache.' Just being able to understand those feelings in our bodies and their impact embodies mindful eating."

Use what you notice in your body to inform mindful eating. There are no right or wrong emotions that influence our eating. Just be aware, if you can. If you struggle with awareness, just take note of that. (*Wow, I feel so rushed right now, I can't even feel my body sensations.*) Noticing that you cannot get in touch with your physical experience still counts as awareness.

Fatigue & Cravings

Mom life is usually spent in some sort of fluctuating level of fatigue. Fatigue presents a potential opportunity to flex our acceptance muscles and mindfulness skills. Why would we bother trying to notice fatigue? Because fatigue is tricky. As you will read about in the sleep chapter (page 105), tiredness wears away our ability to notice our physical experiences. After a night without adequate sleep, we find ourselves searching for quick sources of energy. While most people think of caffeine as the ultimate answer to tiredness, our smart bodies also ask for food sources of quick energy. After a night with a fussy baby, the best-sounding breakfasts probably include pancakes, waffles, or cereal swimming in milk. Carbohydrates and sugar are sources of easily absorbable energy.

In addition to searching for an energy fix, our bodies are also thirsty. Have you had a time where you cannot stop snacking, have a sip of water, and guzzle the whole bottle without realizing your thirst? Thirst can masquerade as hunger. Pile on decreased awareness due to fatigue, and we feel like crazed squirrels foraging through our cabinets.

Emotional Eating

Often clients sheepishly report their difficulties with emotional eating. Bulletin: all eating is emotional in some way or another. Our relationship to food is emotional. Our brains emit hormones that register as an emotional experience when we eat. That's important—it's how our bodies make sure that we don't get bored with eating, forget to do it, and die. Concerning emotional eating behaviors include using food to stuff down, starve away, or manage emotions without addressing them. If this is a pattern for you, connect to support with a therapist or dietitian trained in working with eating disorders.

Sometimes we crave foods physically and emotionally. Just because you wish for an emotional experience of a certain food does not mean this is a bad thing. I urge you to be curious about this craving, fulfill it if helpful, mindfully eat what you want, and honor your fullness. It is unhelpful to pathologize the normal experience of feeling emotional connections with food.

How to Get Food

Now that you know how hungry you are and what you want to eat, you have to go get it. Or someone has to. Shopping can be the worst when you have a baby. It can be even worse with a baby and an older child. I enjoy food shopping and even that was my limit. It can be stressful and feel like it takes hours of planning. I am with you, momma. In this, I offer you a few strategies.

- Keep a running list and use it. Set up a Google doc and grant access permission to your partner, friends, family members, or anyone who offered to lend a hand. If people ask what you need, you won't know when you're in the middle of a feeding while playing PJ Masks with your older child. Just tell them to check the list. If you end up with duplicates, this is a good problem. Many foods can be frozen, stuffed into a cabinet, or donated to those in need. Abundance is not usually an issue that lasts long in the life of a postpartum parent.

- Set a standing order with a grocery delivery service. Yes, I know it can be boring to get the same things every week. Have your pantry and fridge staples automatically delivered. You don't have to subject yourself to recreating the wheel every week by heading to the store with a new list.

- Just shop for today. Shop with your stroller. Get what you need for today and maybe tomorrow morning. Tomorrow is a different day anyway. Who knows what you are going to want? Grant yourself permission to get just what you need.

- Bring a helper. No, I don't mean your other child, unless they are a legitimate help. if people offer to help, ask them to meet you at the grocery store. Have them push the stroller while you shop.

- Get takeout. Let someone else cook. I know it feels like you've had more takeout than you've ever had in your life. It's okay. This is also the craziest year of your life.

Many of us forget what a privilege it is to have ready access to food. I would be remiss without addressing those situations where there is not enough food to go around for a mom and her family. In 2017, Dr. Carolyn Black Becker and her research team conducted a survey of 503 participants examining the relationship between food insecurity and eating disordered behaviors. Researchers found that "participants with the highest level of food insecurity (i.e., adults who reported having hungry children in their household) also endorsed significantly higher levels of binge eating, overall eating disorder pathology, dietary restraint, weight self-stigma, and worry compared to participants with lower levels of food insecurity. Overall, 17 percent of those in the child hunger food insecurity group reported clinically significant eating disorder pathology." For those of us who do not speak "eating disorder researcher," allow me to speak plainly. The people in the study who most worried about having enough food in the house to feed their families were most likely to display eating disordered behaviors. An estimated 1 in 8 Americans, including 11 million children, live with food insecurity.

Finding assistance when dealing with food insecurity:

- Visit the Women, Infant & Children's supplemental nutrition WIC website https://www.fns.usda.gov/wic/wic-how-apply and Supplemental Nutrition Assistance Program website https://www.fns.usda.gov/snap/applicant-recipient to apply for supplemental assistance
- If you receive assistance from the supplemental nutritional assistance program (SNAP), any children in the household qualify for free or reduced fee school lunch program. Visit https://www.fns.usda.gov/school-meals/applying-free-and-reduced-price-school-meals for details.
- Find your local food bank by logging on to https://www.feedingamerica.org/find-your-local-foodbank or https://www.homelessshelterdirectory.org/foodbanks/

Notes

Black Becker, Carolyn, Keesha Middlemass., Brigette Taylor, Francesa Gomez, and Clara Johnson. "Food Insecurity and Eating Disorder Pathology." International Journal of Eating Disorders. Volume 50, Issue 9, September 2017.

Coleman-Jensen, Alisha, Matthew Rabbitt, Christian Gregory, and Anita Singh. United States Department of Agriculture, "Household Food

Security in the United States in 2018." Economic Research Report Number 270. September 2019.

Feeding America. "Understanding Food Insecurity." Last accessed October 18, 2019. https://hungerandhealth.feedingamerica.org/understand-food-insecurity/

Resch, Evelyn. "Evelyn Resch: Mother of Intuitive Eating." Interview by Corinne Crossley and Jessica Foley, *Momma Bites! podcast,* March 14, 2019.

Resch, Evelyn, and Evelyn Tribole. *Intuitive Eating: A Revolutionary Program That Works.* New York: St. Martin's Griffin, 2012.

Rosinger, Asher, Ann-Marie Chang, Orfeu Buxton, Junjuan Li, Shouling Wu, and Xiang Gao. "Short sleep duration is associated with inadequate hydration: cross-cultural evidence from US and Chinese adults."
Sleep, Volume 42, Issue 2, February 2019.

Stenovec, Lindsay. "Lindsay Stenovec: Embodied & Well Mama." Interview by Corinne Crossley and Jessica Foley, *Momma Bites! podcast,* November 12, 2018.

Chapter 6:

No Rest for the Mommy Sleep

"It's just as I feared," Camille says, twisting a curl around her finger. "He doesn't sleep. It sucks. The only way he will sleep is if I nurse him. I know all the sleep books say not to do that, but I can't help it. I'll go crazy if I don't start getting better sleep."

From the earliest months in her pregnancy with her son, our therapy sessions featured her sleep concerns. Camille valued her sleep in a way that is lost on many of us in our younger years. She was the college student whose light was off at 10:30 p.m. Even as a teenager, she put herself to bed at a respectable hour. Here she was facing down her deepest concern for parenthood—a baby that did not sleep.

We will check in with Camille later in this chapter, but you may connect with her predicament. Sleeplessness in the postpartum year is not exactly a world-rocking issue. It is a well-worn (and in my opinion, obnoxious) response to a person announcing their pregnancy to say "well, sleep now, because you never will again."

Other than the initial first weeks with my daughter, the sleep loss I suffered in my postpartum year felt manageable. After a horrendous case of pregnancy-induced insomnia, I was grateful to be able to sleep in longer stretches and felt able to run on very little sleep.

My postpartum year with my son was a different story.

I was unprepared for how edgy and crazed I felt at night, craving the sleep his cries interrupted. With the two kids sharing a room, I was unwilling to let him put himself back to sleep as I had with my daughter, instead racing into his room at every cry, concerned he would wake his sister. One night, in my sleep-deprived desperation, I recalled the words of the infant care instructor in the class I took before having my daughter. "Remember, sleep deprivation is a type of torture. Do you know the most effective way prisoners of war are kept awake to induce sleep deprivation? Recordings of crying babies. Humans are wired to respond to babies' cries. It penetrates our sleep to awaken us. It is not something that you can easily get used to—it is supposed to wake you up." Sleep deprivation as torture. I had not fully understood her words until this moment, how lack of sleep can truly feel like we are going crazy.

Sleep deprivation is such a destabilizing experience, there are strict boundaries on how sleep researchers can alter subjects' sleep in the pursuits of study. Dr. Hawley Montgomery-Downs, PhD, is a maternal and pediatric sleep specialist at West Virginia University specializing in studying the effects of maternal sleep loss. "There are some real limits on what we can do to people in terms of messing with their sleep. We have so much evidence that sleep is important that you can't ethically deprive people of sleep for a very long time. I don't have to do that experimentally because there is a group of people who have decided to do this to themselves—they're called postpartum parents. Studying the physiological and behavioral sleep patterns of parents quickly made me realize this is a public health issue, a family leave issue, and a societal well-being issue."

Why Is Sleep So Important?

"You don't know what you got till it's gone."

—Cinderella (the 90s hair metal band, not the Disney princess)

You probably did not consider the importance of sleep before it disappeared from your nights. When I asked Dr. Downs about the importance of sleep, she explained sleep's role as equally important to anything we do in our waking life. "When we sleep, our bodies repair themselves. The brain gets cleaned out. We recharge in numerous different ways. If we do not sleep—in the short term we have dire consequences. In the long term, we die without sleep."

Sleep is not a passive process. Dr. Downs continues: "Sleep prepares us for being more intensively productive and in a better mood. Sleep is critical to things like having a decent reaction time so we can drive safely. Much earlier than sleep researchers were ever looking at this, people who study memory and cognitive abilities were looking at what we lovingly call 'baby brain' and the data to support how our cognitive abilities change after the birth of a child. One of the things that I'm really interested in is how much of that change is due to sleep disturbance. We know there are long-term changes because studying chronic long-term sleep disturbance in animal models shows areas of the brain that morph in ways that do not recover. I worry that we are vulnerable to that phenomenon.

"Additionally, one of the things that we do know is relative to birth spacing. Traditionally, in the Western world, we have our babies around a year and a half apart. We know that women's sleep has recovered by the time they have their next baby, but the effects of sleep deprivation have not worn off. This can cause slower reaction times and memory impairment compared to where we were before the first baby. These are modifiable factors, but to do so, we have to make choices to involve other people in our lives. Not many of us are good at that. The signs are subtle and you lose perspective over time and don't realize that you're not quite where you were."

In the infant years after my children were born, my husband and I both dreaded the extreme turns of the weather in Massachusetts. Both of us sleep-deprived, I obsessed over leaving my baby in a hot car in the summer, while he feared forgetting to clear a tailpipe while warming the car after snowstorms. I left an article on preventing hot car deaths stuck to my fridge. I put my purse in the backseat with my son when I drove him anywhere on my own. I kept his bag for daycare on the seat next to me when I drove him to school. I did not feel I could implicitly trust my under-slept brain. Even years after these dangers have passed, as I interviewed Dr. Downs on a steamy August day, I felt my anxiety levels rising as she discussed this risk among postpartum parents. "One of the things we find in sleep-deprived parents is that they will tend to the baby. They do the necessary things—feed the baby on time, change their diapers, do all of those basics, but they don't respond to the baby's verbal cues as much. They don't look their babies in the eye. They do those spaced-out things that parents worry about without realizing it."

How Tired Are You?

What is enough sleep? How much sleep are we supposed to be getting? When I asked Dr. Downs this most basic of questions, she sighed. "There's a lot of emphasis on providing consensus recommendations for how much sleep different age groups should be getting. But there are huge individual differences. The truth is, when you look at those statistics, there are very large ranges in what is considered normal. People need to focus on how they feel."

Signs of fatigue:
- Falling asleep places other than your bed
- Nodding off at times you don't intend to sleep
- Feeling disproportionately emotional (irritable, upset, sad, etc.)
- Feeling wound-up, unable to sleep (the way kids get when they are overtired)
- Yawning
- Lack of concentration
- Forgetfulness
- Thirst, dehydration, darker urine
- Carbohydrate craving
- Nausea
- Headaches
- Increased hunger

"Listen to your body," Dr. Downs urges. It is easy to miss our signs when we are tired or feel like we are functioning better than we are. "One of the unfortunate aspects of sleep loss and disturbance is how quickly we lose our ability for self-insight. Very much like alcohol intoxication where with a couple of drinks, your perception of how impaired you are gets skewed. The more you drink, the more skewed it gets, to the point where there are people who think they drive better when they're drunk. Sleep loss and disturbance do some of those same things."

Still unsure how far your sleep falls short? If you really want to know how much sleep your body actually needs, Dr. Downs recommends this exercise: "There's this really easy experiment that people can do when their lives allow. I acknowledge that not everyone is in a situation where they can do this. Turn off your alarm, close the shades, and arrange for no one to wake you. When you go to sleep, how long do you sleep? When you are not doing this exercise, how hard is it for you to wake up when the alarm goes off in the morning? People who get enough sleep generally report that they haven't felt this good in years. They didn't think they could feel this way. It's like getting a new lease on life. I feel sort of evil saying this to new moms because everyone's craving that, but as you work through that postpartum process, getting back to that goal of feeling fully recovered is important."

Dr. Downs's experiment might sound about as easy as colonizing Saturn for a summer home, but it is a possible long-term goal to reconnect to feeling sleep-restored at some point. Consider this a baseline to shoot for as your baby sleeps longer stretches of time. Also, this is a helpful incentive for attending to your baby's sleep needs.

But My Fitbit Says I Slept Well . . .

Ah, wearables. How did we know we moved enough, slept enough, or breathed enough before our watches told us? When I asked Dr. Downs about the usefulness of wearables in conjunction with sleep tracking, she responded, "I would rather people stop wearing their devices on their wrists, stop listening to official recommendations, and instead listen to our bodies. I'm super happy that there is an apparent market of people who want to pay attention to that incredibly important health relevant topic. But relying on those devices is ill-advised at best."

Dr. Downs explained that sleep detection by wearables is limited in their technology. "They are simple movement detectors. If you are a really solid sleeper where you're not moving around a lot during the night, and there's no disruption waking you, then your device is going to be fairly accurate.

But, as soon as you start having brief arousals, awakenings, and disturbing aspects to your sleep—these cause micro-arousals, which are damaging to the integrity of sleep. Even for a couple seconds at a time. Those devices don't detect these micro-arousals. So, you can have an absolute miserable night of sleep, and the device on your wrist is going to say you slept great. It's a problem if your device is telling you that you slept better than you did. If it was the opposite, and it was saying you slept terribly when you slept fine, then you would have a false positive. You would be concerned about your sleep but not for any real reason. That's not great, but it's much worse to have a condition where you should be worried about your sleep but you're getting a false sense of security from this thing on your wrist. Giving someone a device that says 'all good, you got great sleep last night,' when you really didn't is a whole lot like giving someone a breathalyzer that says, 'yup, no problem, ready to go,' when they're actually impaired. People who are drunk or really sleep-deprived shouldn't be driving. In those situations, knowing that you're impaired is really important so you can accommodate that."

The Basics of Sleep

What is a sleep cycle? What are the most important parts of our sleep cycle? Dr. Downs gave us some basics on sleep. "All sleep stages are important. They happen in a certain order. Sleep is not like a book. If you're getting into it, get interrupted, then return to sleep, you don't get to pick up where you left off. You have to start back at the beginning. Sleep cycles are about ninety minutes long. When we're awakened a lot (like once an hour), you're getting selectively cut off from those latter stages. The last stage that happens after about forty minutes to an hour into sleep is REM (rapid eye movement) sleep. We used to just think of REM as important because that is when dreams happen. We understand now that it is absolutely critical in terms of memory processing and cognitive abilities; cleaning the brain out, storing short-term to long-term memory, and creativity as well. If we're awakened hourly, we're not giving ourselves the opportunity to get into REM. We end up selectively deprived of that stage."

But REM is not the only important part of our sleep cycle. As Dr. Downs mentioned, all parts of the cycle are important. A particularly vital, earlier part of the cycle is slow-wave sleep. "Slow-wave or delta-wave sleep is when growth hormones and the immune system are doing their very best work. People with sleep-deprivation or sleep-fragmentation tend to have problems with immunity, fighting off diseases."

Sleep Deprivation versus Sleep Fragmentation

I remember the first time my daughter slept six hours in a row. My body awakened and I sensed light coming through the windows. For the first time in an unimaginable stretch, I did not feel ill upon waking. I felt rested. I bolted upright. In only a few strides, I flew down the hall into her room to ascertain that she was still breathing. My heart hammered in my chest, adrenaline blasting out the well-being of the milestone. She lay in her crib, breathing deeply, still ensconced in her delta-wave sleep. Once she (and therefore, I) routinely slept six consecutive hours, I felt like I could do anything. Broker peace talks. Cure cancer. Solve climate change. I felt like I could do it all.

Reiterating this experience to Dr. Downs, she validated my feelings. "It can feel like six is the new eight hours when you have the integrity of the sleep cycle." Here Dr. Downs explains a major distinction that we misunderstand about postpartum sleep loss. "One thing that shocked us about the first study we did in the laboratory was how fragmented moms' sleep really is. We expected to see some combination of interruption plus sleep deprivation. That's an important distinction. Being sleep-deprived means that you're getting less sleep overall. Being sleep-fragmented means the integrity of the sleep cycle is interrupted and you have to start over again. We thought we'd see both and we didn't. There was actually no sleep deprivation. Women in our studies, on average, were getting about seven and a half hours of sleep if you add up all the pieces of it. But there was no integrity to it. It was like taking a normal amount of sleep and chopping it up like confetti. Being sleep-fragmented is just as bad as being sleep-deprived. Even though they were getting enough sleep overall, they felt as though they weren't getting any."

The distinction between sleep fragmentation and deprivation is not necessarily intuitive. We see the numbers on the clock and it doesn't make sense why we're so tired. "I don't know why this is getting to me so much," Camille would say to me in session in the months before she was able to engineer a closer approximation to the sleep she needed. "I'm going to bed at 9:30 and staying in bed until 6:00 a.m.—that should be more than enough!" Here, Camille exemplifies a particular issue that makes challenges like sleep loss so much worse for moms—how hard we are on ourselves. We think we should be doing better than we are. Too often, we get distracted by these judgments rather than tuning into how we feel. Dr. Downs continues, "It's insidious because we think 'I got an hour here, and I got an hour and a half there, and I got another hour there, et cetera, so what's wrong with me?' If somebody had obstructive sleep apnea and they're constantly waking, you wouldn't point to them and say 'Suck it up! Stop being such a loser,' but we do that to ourselves."

I Know I'm Not Getting Enough Sleep—Now What?

You're exhausted. If you have one, your partner is probably exhausted. You need some ideas of how to manage this now. Let's backtrack for a second and consider this—are you a morning or a night person? Since becoming a mother, I am distinctly a morning person. My husband is and has always been a night person. Does this really matter when you are a postpartum parent and all hours of the day and night are up for grabs around a sleeping baby? It does.

Dr. Downs recommends an online survey called the Morningist or Eveningist scale. "Horne and Östberg are scientists who developed a way of looking at sleep and functioning. Informally, 'are you an owl or are you a lark?' Are you an evening or a morning person? We know that after the amount and quality of sleep that you get, the third important element is when you sleep. Having routine sleep times is important from a circadian (our internal clock settings) function. We know that our biologic rhythms happen on about a twenty-four-hour basis, so sleeping at all random times gives you what is affectionately referred to as social jet lag (the discrepancy between how our body wants to sleep versus where sleep fits into our lifestyle). The importance of a schedule prevents that dysregulated feeling."

Even when we intuitively know what time of day our bodies prefer to sleep, this survey is worth taking. In the middle of the night, we forget. We suck it up and just do what needs to be done, even if it is not our intuitive time to be awake. A plan that resists martyrdom supports our long-term physical and relationship health. I remember the first time my husband, the night owl, mistakenly told a family friend that our daughter regularly slept through the night. I fought the urge to pick up a heavy object and swing. Instead, I opted for a passive-aggressive "actually she doesn't, but he does," irritated that I was covering his intuitive time of wakefulness. Dr. Downs reinforces this point: "Knowing whether you're a morning or an evening person can be really helpful to strategize. If you realize *wow, I am totally a night person* and you happen to live with a morning person, you can leverage those strengths. Arrange your shifts with the baby accordingly. The night person can stay up later and do the bedtime routine while the morning person went to bed long ago. It may mean that a couple does not see very much of each other but I am willing to say that it is worth the trade for both to be more well-rested when you do see each other."

Dealing with sleep loss puts us in a chronically reactive state. As Dr. Downs highlighted earlier, we do what needs to be done, but higher thinking is difficult to access. We need to slow down and be direct with what we need. Dr. Downs encourages co-parents to be strategic. "Sit down when you feel like you can be open to think from a creative, problem-solving perspective about what resources you have. What strategies do you have? Some people have big spaces and they can go to a quiet area and get some sleep. Consider, is it really necessary to have the baby monitor turned up full-blast so that you can hear every little hitch in your newborn's breath?" In some cases, being exhausted puts a fine point on long-term parenting values. Consider your values in managing this issue of sleep. "Will the baby co-sleep? In which case, how will you make this the safest area possible? Are you both on board with breastfeeding? Can you come up with strategies so that the person who is not breastfeeding can give a bottle of expressed milk at certain times? Come up with different techniques that your family chooses to do," Dr. Downs offers.

All I Need Is a Little Nap . . .

What about napping? (For moms, not their babies.) What about that adage, "Sleep when the baby sleeps"? "If someone experiences a twenty-minute nap during the day and they feel good as a result, I'm not going to disparage that. I encourage them to use whatever time and resources are available to them," Dr. Downs offers. "But the truth is, there are very few postpartum women who feel that way. Instead, what we tend to do is not nap, then write thank-you cards, do laundry, and the zillion things that need doing, and then we beat ourselves up for it. That nap probably wouldn't have done you that much good anyway. Although I feel a bit squeamish about saying 'don't worry about sleeping,' the truth is, you'd be better off sitting down and using that time contacting loved ones saying, 'I need three hours of sleep tonight, can you please come over and take the eleven o'clock feeding.' Strategies like that with whatever resources are at people's disposal."

Dr. Downs continues: "There is not one among us that does not think at two o'clock in the morning, *How does anyone survive this? How has the human species made it through this? How has anyone survived to evolve? Because this is horrible.* The truth is we haven't been doing this for millennia. The way we do it now is a modern invention. As a society, we uniquely created this social self-isolation where a couple raises a baby by themselves. I have moms who are single by choice that are so far ahead of the average mainstream couple in insuring they and their infant are well-cared for by a large group of people. That's the way we all ought to be doing it."

Get Help

Sleep may not seem like something we're supposed to ask for help with. When people offer to help, it may feel okay to have them move the laundry from the washer to the dryer, bring by a dish, or drop off groceries. But sleep feels like a bridge too far. And yet, it really is one of the most important. If you have trouble accepting help, consider allowing yourself to ask for support with getting some serious sleep during the daytime or early morning.

Remember Camille? Have you been wondering about her since the beginning of the chapter? Before I ever spoke with Dr. Downs and learned some of these interventions, Camille figured out some things intuitively. She traded shifts with her husband who was an owl (night person) to her lark (morning person) and expressed milk for him to cover feedings. She kept the monitor out of the room while she slept and he was on duty. While they grew testy with one another at times with their limited time together as a couple, their resilience improved with increased sleep. When she saw the difference that this made for her, she began to consider the value of sleep-training now that her baby was older. She agonized over timing and methods in session for weeks. I reassured her that whatever direction they determined was up to them and had to fit with their needs and values.

She scoured the Internet for a sleep-training program she and her husband could stomach. She connected to support for managing the heartbreaks of sleep training, which was hard on her at times, but she found it instrumental for getting the sleep she needed. While her son was far from a perfect sleeper, everyone's outlook improved with increased sleep.

Notes

Keifer, Tom. "Don't Know What You Got (Till It's Gone)." On Long Cold Winter. Chicago, Il: Mercury Records, 1988, compact disc.

Montgomery-Downs, Hawley. "Sleepless Survival Strategies with Hawley Montgomery-Downs." Interview by Corinne Crossley, *Momma Bites! podcast*, September 4, 2019.

Chapter 7:

More Than Just the Blues

Postpartum Mood Disorders

"With my first son, I had postpartum depression and anxiety," Lindsay tells me in a *Momma Bites!* podcast interview. Lindsay Stenovec, RD, is the host of *The Embodied & Well Mom Show* and the owner of Nutrition Instincts in San Diego, California. "I did not realize what was going on until fourteen months after he was born. When I think back about the postpartum period with my first son, it's pretty painful. While we had a connection, my memory is fuzzy of this time. It took me a long time to realize that I was experiencing PPD and PPA (postpartum depression and postpartum anxiety). I kept thinking *this will get better, I'm overreacting, I'm sure I'm fine.*" Over and over in the course of writing this book, I heard moms, including experts in the field of postpartum mood disorders, report how they put off treatment by telling themselves 'it will get better,' but it didn't.

Once an unspeakable condition, the word "postpartum" now rarely stands without mention of its typical partner "depression." Whenever I discussed writing this book, inevitably people assumed it would primarily address mood disorders. In 2005, when Brooke Shields bravely wrote in her memoir *Down Came the Rain* about her authentic experience of postpartum depression, she was both lauded and lambasted about her disclosure. Since sharing her story, many of Hollywood's elite ranging from Chrissy Teigen to Courteney Cox spoke out about their experience of struggles with postpartum mood and anxiety disorders (PMADs).

But what is postpartum depression? Postpartum anxiety? Are they the same as the baby blues? How do they differ from other mood disorders? Will I get better? These questions burn on the minds of new moms.

Baby Blues

Many providers drop the phrase "baby blues" with little explanation of what they are and how they differ from postpartum mood disorders. This was one of the first questions I had for Jessica Foley, LMHC, psychotherapist in the Boston area specializing in treating postpartum mood disorders (and occasional cohost of the *Momma Bites!* podcast). "I explain it to moms as a spectrum. At the very outskirts of that spectrum is the baby blues. They are normal and a typical part of early motherhood. According to the Postpartum Support International website, about eighty percent of women have this experience. Baby blues usually happen rapidly—about three to five days after giving birth. We are learning how this experience relates to hormones. When we're talking about the difference between the baby blues and PPD/PPA, the main things we want to focus on are how often and how much. For example, we want to know the duration—how long it's happening. For some moms, this might look like moments three to five days after birth where you're crying at commercials or feeling overwhelmed. If that is relieved when you talk about it, cry about it, or goes away over the next few days (usually one to two weeks total) we're talking baby blues. If it's persisting and/or getting worse, then we consider that on the spectrum of postpartum depression or anxiety." In her seminal text *This Isn't What I Expected: Overcoming Postpartum Depression*, Karen Kleiman, LCSW, and Valarie Raskin, MD, likewise describe baby blues in this vein: "The sadness and crying come and go, are interspersed with periods of serenity and pleasure, and can usually be shaken off with support, a nap, or by getting out of the house" (Kleiman & Raskin 2013, 13).

What are PMADs?

"People call it lots of different names. Most commonly we hear postpartum depression as an umbrella term for many different things," Jessica attests. In fact, the term postpartum depression is such a misnomer that many mothers struggle to recognize their postpartum anxiety as a mood disorder that warrants attention. So vigilant for depression, women dealing with other postpartum mood disorders miss symptoms.

How can we tell if we are dealing with a postpartum mood disorder? How do they differ from the "garden variety" mood disorders that some of us dealt with in our lives before baby? "The biggest difference is the timing—postpartum onset," Jessica informs. "It's such a complex picture because the more typical indicators we would look for in depression would be fairly normal in a new mom. You're not sleeping? Of course, you're not sleeping! So, we need to phrase questions a little differently. For example, we might ask 'If you have the opportunity to sleep, are you able to fall asleep?' A new mom who wasn't experiencing postpartum depression or anxiety would say 'Heck yeah, I can sleep when I'm standing at the sink!'"

Rather than considering postpartum mood disorders as a collection of totally different disorders isolated from one another, Jessica returns to her spectrum explanation. "On one side you have those women who present as more classically depressed—trouble getting out of bed, no appetite, or over-eating. Also on that spectrum is anxiety. At the extreme edge are OCD-type symptoms like obsessional or impulsive symptoms. Women can fall any-where in that range. It's pretty rare for women to fall outside that spectrum. Actually, it's pretty rare that I see a client fall exclusively into postpartum depression. Most moms get a dose of both depression and anxiety. Most of the moms I see are ambitious, type A, well-educated, and have their shit together as moms. But they are anxious as hell."

"Because it is such an umbrella term, the media gives us a pretty inaccurate picture of PPD. When people think about the heavy cases in the news of harm to moms or children—that's postpartum psychosis, which is a totally different animal. In the eleven years where I've treated women, I saw that once. It's very rare. But moms can feel scared to ask for help or acknowledge their feelings in fear they will be associated with this type of disorder," Jessica states.

Symptoms of postpartum depression (according to Postpartum Support International):

- Anger or irritability
- Lack of interest in baby or baby care
- Lack of appetite or alternately overeating/bingeing/compulsive eating
- Difficulty sleeping
- Difficulty getting out of bed

- Crying or pervasive sadness
- Lack of concentration
- Feelings of guilt, shame, or hopelessness
- Loss of interest in things you used to enjoy
- Thoughts of hurting yourself or your baby

Symptoms of postpartum anxiety (according to Postpartum Support International):

- Persistent worry
- Dread or feeling that something bad is going to happen
- Racing thoughts
- Lack of appetite or alternately overeating
- Difficulty sleeping
- Inability to sit still
- Dizziness, hot flashes, and nausea
- Fear of leaving home or being alone

Symptoms of postpartum stress syndrome (according to *This Isn't What I Expected: Overcoming Postpartum Depression*):

- Anxiety
- Self-doubt
- Wishing to be a perfect mother
- Unrealistic expectations
- Feelings of inadequacy
- Helplessness
- Sense of disappointment in oneself and new role/life
- Desire to be in control at all times
- Despite internal experience, functioning well (getting what needs to be done completed)
- Symptoms are less severe than clinical depression

Symptoms of postpartum panic disorder:

- Difficulty breathing, feeling like you cannot catch your breath or control your breathing
- Heart racing
- Chest pain
- Profuse sweating
- Chills, dizziness, numbness, tingling, or nausea
- Feeling like you are going to die
- Feeling like you are going crazy or losing control

Symptoms of postpartum obsessive-compulsive disorder (according to Postpartum Support International):

- Obsessions or intrusive thoughts
- Persistent or repetitive upsetting thoughts or mental images related to the baby
- Obsessions are not something that you have experienced in the past
- Compulsions (doing certain things over and over again to reduce fears and obsessions)
- Constant need to clean, check things many times, count or reorder things
- A sense of horror about the obsessions
- Fear of being left alone with the infant
- Hypervigilance in protecting the infant

Please note that most moms with postpartum OCD know that their thoughts are bizarre and are very unlikely to ever act on them.

In their book *This Wasn't What I Expected: Overcoming Postpartum Depression*, Karen Kleiman and Valarie Raskin, MD, explain: "Postpartum OCD is probably the most under-detected and undertreated of the anxiety disorders that follow childbirth, in part because women are embarrassed and reluctant to reveal what they are thinking." They continue "postpartum depression and OCD often coexist, but many women, as well as their doctors, focus on the depressive symptoms" (Kleiman & Raskin 2013, 20). As hard as it is, if you're having these thoughts and feelings, please connect with your provider and speak up about your experience.

Postpartum post-traumatic stress disorder (as defined in Kleiman and Raskin's book):

- Distressing thoughts or images of past traumatic events
- Avoidance of potential trauma triggers
- Hypervigilance in protection of self or baby
- Lashing out or other angry responses that feel beyond your control
- Exaggerated startle responses

Postpartum psychosis (as defined by Postpartum Support International):

- Delusions or strange beliefs
- Hallucinations (seeing or hearing things that aren't there)
- Feeling very irritated
- Hyperactivity
- Decreased need for or inability to sleep
- Paranoia and suspiciousness
- Rapid mood swings
- Difficulty communicating at times
- History or family history of bipolar disorder or psychotic episodes

While this condition is extremely rare, any of these symptoms warrant immediate attention and intervention. If you or someone you know is experiencing these types of symptoms, reach out for help immediately.

The Triggering Nature of Motherhood

"Motherhood is this experience that puts the magnifying glass on any piece of our lives that might be slightly off or triggering in some way. We can't just give people happy-go-lucky messages. That's going to work for a certain percentage of the people, but that leaves the rest of us women wondering 'Why doesn't that work for me?'"

—Courtney Wyckoff, founder of Momma Strong

"I have this idea for a book called 'Parenting is triggering as fuck,'" Divya tells me in our interview. Divya Kumar, LCSW, CLC, former postpartum doula, lactation counselor, and co-founder of the Perinatal Mental Health Alliance for People of Color (as well as several other vital programs), is a psychotherapist specializing in perinatal mental health, trauma, and anti-oppression work. Basically, a complete badass. "When I ran new parent groups where I acknowledged how triggering parenting can be, I felt everybody in the room exhale like they had been holding their breath forever. The hard things we've experienced in our lives, be it abuse in the home, sexual trauma, eating disorders, bullying, race-based trauma, learning disabilities, all that shit is with us. We carry it in us. Ideally, it's not our whole story, but when you're tired, feel broken, your baby is crying *again*, and your body is not yours—that's where all of our self-regulation skills gets messed with."

But what is a trigger? How do I know when I'm getting triggered? Divya explains: "A trigger is something in the present eliciting a somatic (or body) memory/reaction rooted in a past trauma or upsetting event. You're having a reaction to something now that's based on something that happened before." Divya illustrates with an example from her own life. "I remember going to a moms' group I adored. I was getting ready to nurse my son and I suddenly had the thought *my body looks different than everyone here*. I was looking for another woman of color in the room and thinking *are my breasts the only brown breasts in the room?* I had to step back and think *why am I suddenly thinking this*? It was this weird moment of being in a room of white women triggering memories of racial trauma and punishment for having a different body. I had this flash of *my brown breasts are different!* When we're postpartum, our bodies are so exposed. Once I realized what was going on, I could acknowledge it and move on enough to nurse my baby."

Divya continues. "Our mental health is so cumulative. It's hard to parse out which pieces contribute to PMADs. All the stuff we carry adds to the overall load. Just the things we do in daily baby care can be triggering. Issues with food or disordered eating? That shit is going to come up every sixty to ninety minutes. We're feeding our babies twelve times in twenty-four hours. It's relentless. Even if you have a lot of skills, we get overloaded." She elucidates with examples. "What if you have chronic sleep disruptions because of trauma? Not being able to sleep is going to be really hard for you. Not to mention, sexual trauma with the experience of being touched all the time and having medical exams with our body parts out. Or the experience of raising brown children and being in the grocery store where people say 'Are you her mom or her nanny?' My son has brown skin while my daughter's is more olive. People would ask 'Are you the babysitter?'"

Knowing our triggers is important, but does not necessarily keep them from happening. As Divya explains in her nursing experience, the trigger came out of nowhere and took her a moment to understand. While she managed it, the experience was powerful enough to recall over a decade later. Acknowledging our emotional vulnerability during this period is important. Apologies for your feelings are neither necessary or appropriate. Be it life-change overwhelm, postpartum mood disorder brain chemistry, or trauma trigger, it all counts. None are right or wrong experiences. All require self-care and support.

When do PMADs show up?

This Isn't What I Expected: Overcoming Postpartum Depression authors Kleiman and Raskin explain: "PPD usually occurs one to three months after childbirth. However, PPD can emerge any time, from immediately following the birth of the baby until a year after" (Kleiman & Raskin 2013, 10). Jessica Foley expands on this. "Typically, moms go in for their checkup six weeks after they had their baby and receive what looks like a pop-quiz called the Edinburgh. It's pretty short, doesn't give a ton of information, and has very black-or-white answers. It doesn't leave a lot of leeway for you to say 'Well, sometimes I feel this way, but 99 percent of the time I feel this other way.' A lot of the time, providers don't really explain the Edinburgh, it's handed to you in a packet of other paperwork. Since it's not really explained, some moms feel *Oh god, this is where they're going to find out I'm crazy and take away my baby. I'm going to tell them I'm perfectly fine.* Because of this we need to explain the Edinburgh better. We also need to get moms in sooner. Lots of practices moved toward a three-week visit protocol, which makes so much more sense for mental and physical health. The other opportunity where people might get diagnosed is at their pediatrician's office. The pediatrician is probably going to be the first appointment that you have after you have a baby and the Edinburgh is often there as well. Generally, moms get diagnosed or referred to a mental health provider usually around six weeks."

"As for the top range of PMADs onset," Jess continues, "I've heard varying things including up to after a year. It's a pretty big range. Initially, there can be a lot of misguidance of whether a mood disorder is PMAD-related. I often see moms who say 'Now looking back, I think I had it.'"

Risk Factors of PMADs

- Past trauma
- Past incidences of anxiety or depression
- Traumatic birth experiences
- Traumatic pregnancy experiences
- A baby in the NICU
- Cesarean section
- Family history of mood disorders or postpartum mood disorders

- Financial or relationship stress
- History of PMS or premenstrual dysphoric disorder
- Thyroid imbalances
- Inadequate support
- Birth of multiples (twins, etc.)
- Predisposition to self-criticism
- Recent major life transition (move, loss, etc.)
- Single parenting without significant support
- Lack of or difficulty with access to care

Jessica advises "This is not a situation where we can say 'you have x, so you're definitely going to get y' but rather 'you're more likely to perhaps develop this condition.' If we can start identifying women before giving birth and provide the option of increased support via early establishment of relationships with mental health providers, it increases the chances we can catch something sooner."

"Because we're not taking good care of African-American moms in this country, this is another risk factor we must address," Jess informs. According to the Center for American Progress, rates of postpartum mood disorders are nearly 20 percent higher in women of color, yet 60 percent report not receiving any services related to this issue. Divya cites on her website: "The rates of perinatal emotional complications are nearly twice as high among low-income women and women of color, compared to white, middle class women; yet, women in these populations receive screening and treatment for emotional complications at much lower rates." In our interview, Divya added: "The tricky thing is a lot of the research conflates race and class. Much of the research is on low-income women of color. We need so much more research to really parse out what is race versus access to resources. For example, there was a diaper study done out of Yale that found lack of access to a steady diaper supply can increase rates of anxiety and depression."

"At the same time," Divya continues, "when we look at the toxic effects of weathering, we see those effects at much higher rates in higher-incomes brackets." What is weathering? Think of it as erosion, but for humans. People of color are under the constant stress of both overt and implied racism in daily life. Only in the last decade has research evolved to prove what so many already knew in their bones—racism is harming health in people of color. Not just mental health. Physical health. In 2006, the American Journal of Public Health published the findings of Arline Geronimus and her research partners demonstrating that Black women topped the list of those with highest rates of allostatic load (read, damage to their bodies). "The disparities in birth outcomes between white women and black women in the highest income brackets are actually wider than in lower income brackets. So, it's not just access to care," Divya continues. "Perceived racism is causing toxicity and damage. When we think about disenfranchisement, we must acknowledge the many barriers to disclosing struggles. Whether its access to care, lack of services in your language, transportation, cultural stigma (e.g., 'We don't really talk about this stuff' or 'We don't go to mental health providers'), there can be a real lack of trust in the medical system. Imagine feeling fearful of reporting depression due to worry DCF will to come take your baby. And even if you do say something, does the provider take your insurance? Speak your language? Do you have transportation? Admitting to perinatal emotional complications, let alone access to treatment—is a privilege," Divya says.

Treatment for PMADs

"I want moms to know, if the thought *is this postpartum depression?* comes into your head over and over, go see someone! People who aren't suffering from it probably aren't asking themselves that question. If you are suffering, even if it doesn't fit into a diagnosis, go see someone. Once I got into therapy, I did a lot of work. I went on medication for a short time and learned so much about myself. I now have a much wider threshold of tolerance for my emotions. I have so much more insight. So, the second time when I experienced my mood dipping again between three to six months postpartum, I knew within days what was happening. I realized it wasn't my fault and knew where to go to get help. I got in to see a therapist right away and I continue that work because it is so helpful. I can be more present with the discomforts and with the really great times as well."

—Lindsay Stenovec, RD, host of *The Embodied & Well Mom* podcast

Referral sources for a qualified PMADs provider (therapist or medication provider):

- Ob/gyn or midwife
- Pediatrician's office
- Postpartum doula or lactation consultant
- Postpartum support international
- The Postpartum Stress Center

Types of Treatment
Therapy

"It's amazing to see how quickly people tend to recover and how much better they feel. Whereas when I'm treating other types of issues, the progress can feel much slower. Sometimes just a few days difference in a mom is very impactful," Jessica shares. Therapists come with all sorts of trainings and qualifications. Looking for providers can be a bit of alphabet soup. Any of the following have completed adequate education and licensure to provide therapy (additional training on PMADs is done on postgraduate level):

- PhD
- PsyD
- LICSW/LCSW (Licensed Clinical Social Worker)
- LMHC (Licensed Mental Health Counselor)
- LMFT (Licensed Marriage and Family Therapist)

Following are just a few types of psychotherapy that can be helpful in treating PMADs:

Cognitive behavioral therapy: "The gold standard is CBT, which can be helpful because when we're feeling depressed or anxious, our thoughts get in the way," Jessica explains. "Also, this can be a powerful tool to challenge unhelpful thoughts such as myths of motherhood like *I should be able to do this on my own.*"

Dialectical behavioral therapy: Focused on managing the experience of powerful emotions, DBT offers skills in mindfulness, emotion regulation, interpersonal effectiveness, and distress tolerance.

Eye Motion Desensitization Reprocessing (EMDR): For those dealing with acute trauma responses, EMDR offers helpful tools to manage triggering events. This can be an adjunct treatment independent of or in addition to traditional psychotherapy.

Group therapy: No one understands like those going through the same thing as you at the same time as you. Group therapy can take many different forms from psychoeducational, general support, or specific skills-based treatment.

A final word from Jess on this issue: "The type of treatment is not as important as finding a provider you connect with that has experience with postpartum mood disorders."

Medication

Medication can be such a sticky issue for many moms. While they know that they are struggling and want to feel better, they have concerns. Breastfeeding moms worry about how taking medication affects their baby or their ability to nurse. "I'm a big supporter of medication," Jessica reports after years of working with mothers. "Most of the moms I see are on a combination of low dose of a daily medication and, for a brief period of time, an anti-anxiety medication taken as needed, usually to help with sleep." The decision to take medication is a personal one and is best made in collaboration with a psychiatric provider versed in maternal mental health. Your doctor or therapist have resources for these providers. Remember, if you are unsure of whether or not you are ready to try medication, there is no obligation in meeting with a psychiatric provider to consider whether this is an appropriate step in your recovery.

Potential prescribers could include:
- MD: medical doctor
- NP: nurse practitioner
- PNP: psychiatric nurse practitioner

First Sessions

If you have never been to therapy, attending your first session can feel intimidating. Even if this is not your first therapy rodeo, treating PMADs may look different from past sessions. Jessica explains, "In the beginning, depending on severity, therapy will be once or twice a week to establish connection and get some real assistance. This might look more like case management with focus on supports and self-care. We look at your support network and how to tap into resources. In general, your first session with a therapist is going to be centered around taking history and understanding the present. I really want to know what has happened in these past few weeks—how you're sleeping and feeding yourself. At the end of my first sessions, I assign self-care like taking a walk, getting rest, or sending someone on an errand for you. I task my clients with asking for help and examining their needs for the immediate future."

Psychiatric or medication initial sessions

Often people do not understand the difference between a therapist and a prescriber, let alone how their initial sessions contrast. Jessica explains, "A psychiatric intake is more symptom-focused. They're looking at the acuity of specific symptoms from a medical standpoint and alleviating those symptoms with medication. I think moms have to weigh out decisions about medication. We are taught about the importance of breastfeeding, so many moms are leery about putting anything in their body, so we need to help moms make the best decision for them."

Words of Hope

Jessica urges struggling moms to seek help as soon as possible. "Without help, I've seen moms well into their second year, still feeling terrible. On the other side, with treatment, moms get better pretty quickly. Anecdotally, the moms that I see, within three to four weeks, are feeling much better upon getting help."

When I asked Divya what she wished she could offer herself during her postpartum year, she touched my heart with her response. "I had such debilitating anxiety and OCD, I really thought that I was going to die. I felt like I couldn't go on, that I would never feel better, I would never be well, I would never be a good mother. I remember the words of a lactation consultant I loved. A lot of my anxiety centered on breastfeeding. I'd tell her 'I think this is the end.' And she would say to me, "The story is long; the final chapters have not been written.' This is one long story. This is a blip. This isn't who you are. This is not the whole story. This is part of the story."

Notes

Foley, Jessica. "Postpartum Mood Disorders: More Than Just the Baby Blues."
Interview by Corinne Crossley, *Momma Bites! podcast*, January 2020.
Geronimus, Arline, Margaret Hicken, Danya Keene, and John Bound.
"Weathering" and Age Patterns of Allostatic Load Scores Among Blacks and Whites in America." American Journal of Public Health, 96 (5) May 2006.
Demby, Gene. "Making the Case that Discrimination Is Bad for Your Health."
NPR.org, January 14, 2018. https://www.npr.org/sections/codeswitch/2018

/01/14/577664626/

making-the-case-that-discrimination-is-bad-for-your-health

Kleiman, Karen, and Valerie Raskin. *This Isn't What I Expected: Overcoming Postpartum Depression*. Boston: Da Capo Press, 2013.

Kumar, Divya. "Postpartum Health and Racial Inequity." Interview by Corinne Crossley, *Momma Bites! podcast,* February 2020.

Stenovec, Lindsay. "Lindsay Stenovec: Embodied & Well Mama." Interview by Corinne Crossley and Jessica Foley, *Momma Bites! podcast,* November 12, 2018.

Chapter 8:

Sweating for Sanity

Exercise as Postpartum Support

"This isn't even my dog," Courtney says to the camera, mid-plank, referring to the persistent barking in the exercise video. Laughing, I look up from my mat to the laptop on my couch as I attempt to follow an exercise video the likes of which I have never seen. The instructor on the screen appears the culturally dominant model of fitness. Blond, cheerful, and fit-looking. This image is where the similarities with every other fitness video end. She is not on a studio set. There is no music. Her mat is set up in a clear area of her home, not far from laundry machines. Children meander through the camera shot asking her about the location of various belongings. They climb on her, try out moves with her, and hold up cats to the camera. When they whine that something is too hard to do on their own, she calmly tells them, "It's okay, you can do hard things." Where I would have lost my patience, stopped the camera, stomped around the house filling requests before starting over for a more perfect take, she keeps her cool and persists in her self-care. I was instantly in love with Momma Strong.

Momma Strong is a website and fitness movement focused on mothers' particular movement needs. The workouts are fifteen minutes and primarily involve routine household items. As Courtney demonstrates a variety of moves, she also chats to the camera about Momma Strong's central tenets such as 'winning ugly' and 'showing up' which echo the concepts of 'good enough mothering' (as discussed in Chapter 3 on page 47). In Momma Strong lingo, winning ugly is showing up as we are, however we are.

"There is an unpredictable, athletic nature of motherhood," Courtney Wyckoff, founder of Momma Strong explains in our *Momma Bites!* podcast interview. "Unfortunately, we don't train women that motherhood is an athletic venture. Instead we treat it as this thing that happens and not that big of a deal. The reality is that motherhood is extraordinarily physical on a daily basis in a way that is unpredictable, and requires a lot of dynamic movement. My perspective is let's challenge women through all these movements to prepare them for the experience of motherhood." Courtney knows acutely of what she speaks.

Courtney's Story

"The truth is, for me, this stuff comes from my own desperation in trying to solve a problem. Had I been out to create a business, it wouldn't have worked. I was out to solve a problem and was in a lot of pain," she says, sharing her story of Momma Strong's inception. "After my first child was born, I was in tons and tons of pain. I was a Pilates teacher and had to go back to working full time. That was hard on my body. Then I was living this weird, fake life of core strength and yet, nothing I was teaching was helping my body. Meanwhile, my belly was hanging out, things weren't working right, and I was home trying to do things like P90X or those crazy ab insanity workouts without telling anybody."

"That went on for five years until my second child was born. When she was born, my pain got that much worse. Also, the postpartum depression I experienced with my first intensified as well. I was really depressed. I was just lying on the couch all day long. I was in so much pain. Out of a place of desperation, I started doing some research on spines and people who thought differently about back pain. What happened next was two fold. One, I started to see there was another issue going on in my body. I learned that some workouts can do harm and that I had to exercise entirely differently. Rather than flexion, we actually need to strengthen our bodies in extension. Once I found this out for myself, I brought it to my clients. I saw that people wanted a different workout every day. People wanted workouts that were about fifteen minutes. And people needed to be able to show up just as they were, without having to do anything extra. From that, the idea of 'winning ugly' became really important. It was never something mission-directed at the beginning, it was just desperation, a willingness to find a solution, and the decision that I could heal and find a way back into movement."

Courtney's story of disconnection from her body and chronic pain unfortunately are not uncommon. Our bodies are so alien to us after having babies, and yet there is little other advice on how to reacquaint ourselves with these new bodies other than directives to lose the baby weight. This is not what we need. Moms need tools for getting back into our bodies rather than struggling against them.

As an eating disorder and body image specialist, the women I see in my practice spend years focusing on exercise exclusively for weight loss. Doing so results in lack of consistency. Exercise is always associated with drudgery. They make enemies with elliptical machines and dread treadmills. There is no sense of enjoyable options to move. Yet, in further conversation, almost every person who experiences this fractured relationship with exercise and their body, is also able to name a source of movement they enjoy. "Well, I love taking a walk in the woods because I like being close to nature;" "Swimming is fun because it makes me feel like I'm a kid again;" "The great thing about biking is feeling the wind in my face," they tell me as they disparage themselves for not going to the gym.

Why Exercise?

If we want to reap the benefits of exercise, we need to uncouple it from weight loss and appearance-focus. Why exercise if not to change your body shape? I reached out to Associate Professor of Kinesiology at the University of Alberta, Canada, Margie Davenport, PhD, to help answer this question. She directs the Program for Pregnancy and Postpartum Health, a multi-site research program conducting research to improve the lifelong health of pregnant and postpartum women and their children. "We know that physical activity is essential across lifespan for health and well-being, but we strongly believe that this is particularly important in the postpartum period. Research demonstrates the mental health, cardiovascular, and metabolic benefits of postpartum exercise."

Exercise for Mental Health

Even more important to the well-being of new moms are the potential mental health benefits of exercise. Dr. Davenport explains, "We know that PPD affects up to 22 percent of women in the first year after delivery. And even if they don't have clinical depression, we know that up to half of postpartum women experience some type of depressive symptom." For women reluctant to take medication or lack access to psychotherapy, Dr. Davenport's research sought aids to the standard course of PMADs treatment.

"In non-pregnant populations," she explains, "we know exercise is quite beneficial toward reducing depression and depressive symptoms, but only in the last few years have we started looking at the impact of exercise on post-partum depression. We conducted a review of all available studies examining the effects of exercise on postpartum depression and identified sixteen trials to study from this group. Those trials demonstrated that light-to-moderate physical exercise actually improved the severity of mild-to-moderate depressive symptoms. It was also found to increase the likelihood of resolving these symptoms." Said plainly, exercise was not just a nice add-on in this study, but rather, in itself a helpful source of treatment for the participants.

"I just don't think Brooke could've done this. Exercise gives you endorphins. Endorphins make you happy. Happy people don't shoot their husbands. They just don't."
—Elle Woods, *Legally Blonde*

It is no secret that exercise helps release endorphins (the brain chemical that promotes a sense of well-being). In an April 2013 article in the Harvard Medical School newsletter, Associate Professor of Psychiatry Dr. Michael Craig-Miller described brain changes consistent with sustained low-intensity exercise. "In people who are depressed, neuroscientists have noticed that the hippocampus in the brain—the region that helps regulate mood—is smaller. Exercise supports nerve cell growth in the hippocampus, improving nerve cell connections, which helps relieve depression. The mental benefits of aerobic exercise have a neurochemical basis. Exercise reduces levels of the body's stress hormones, such as adrenaline and cortisol. It also stimulates the production of endorphins, chemicals in the brain that are the body's natural pain-killers and mood elevators. Endorphins are responsible for the "runner's high" and for the feelings of relaxation and optimism that accompany many hard workouts after your exercise is over."

Many of my clients heal their relationships with exercise through this felt experience. For the first time in decades, they note feeling brighter and more positive with movement. Conversely, with consistent practice, they notice irritability without adequate movement. Knowing how much better they feel is the major motivator for consistency. This is the direct opposite of exercising for weight loss, which is short-lived and discouraging.

Exercise for Healing Our Relationship to Our Bodies

Improving our mental health by changing our brain chemicals is one thing, but changing our relationship with our bodies is quite another. When we arrive in the postpartum period, our bodies can feel like total strangers to us. Not only have we endured incredible changes in a very short time, our bodies feel co-opted by our babies. This strangeness makes sensing our bodies difficult. Stress, lack of sleep, and inadequate nourishment all decrease our body awareness. Feeling disconnected from our body and its signals worsens our body esteem (feelings about our body). An essential part of improving our body esteem is connecting to and respecting our body sensations.

In our *Momma Bites!* podcast interview, Anna Guest-Jelley, founder and creator of Curvy Yoga, described the ways movement changed both her body awareness and esteem. "It wasn't something that happened overnight. For years I would hear yoga teachers say 'notice what is happening in your back . . . or your breath . . . or your big toe' or whatever, and I always thought 'that's hilarious, they only talk in metaphors.' Then one day I realized they weren't talking in metaphor! People were feeling this the whole time. It took me that long to realize it. The more that I could feel in my body, the more I felt like I was developing a relationship—a conversation that contributed to how I felt about my body. It's something I'm always developing. There's new levels of sensation available to me over time."

Anna describes her journey into yoga as an unlikely one. "It's hard to over-estimate how *not* sporty I was," she says, laughing. "Looking back, it's so funny to me that I found yoga. It was not on my radar in any way. It just fell into my lap. When I was in my junior year of high school, I had a migraine every day." Anna shared that despite her attempts at treatment with Western medicine, nothing worked to alleviate her pain. However, she became intrigued by the concept of treating migraines with biofeedback. Biofeedback is a practice of relaxation techniques with the intention of causing physical changes (muscle relaxation, alteration of heart rate, breathing) to alter one's experience (especially of pain). Anna found through practicing biofeedback that her migraines, though still present, became less frequent. She continued the search for pain management at college and began experimenting with meditation and then yoga. When her roommate was out of their room, Anna practiced alongside a Rodney Yee video. While it was helpful, Anna states that "a lot of it did not work for my body."

Despite her challenges with the video's cues, Anna's appreciation for yoga grew until she ventured out to find a class. Since yoga was not part of the cultural zeitgeist it is today, finding a class was difficult. "When practicing in these classes, I felt the instructions meant that I'd really get it once I lost weight." Landing in a class where she was the youngest student by a couple of decades allowed her to be curious and adapt her practice to her body. Anna began to realize, "My body had not been the problem in yoga, they just had not learned how to teach bodies like mine. I think most yoga teachers are well-intentioned and mean it when they say their classes are for everyone. But having that intention in your heart is not the same as having the skills to back that up."

Anna continued to practice yoga and experiment with different postures, developing a vast array of modifications for poses. "I just thought I cannot be the only bigger-bodied person who wants this information." She was right. In 2010, Curvy Yoga was born from years of healing and experimentation. In the years since realizing her teachers were not talking in metaphor, Anna cultivated a curiosity and practice of listening to her body that spawned an entire yoga practice. "I believe in my bones that any person can do yoga, it's just a matter of making the pose work for them. A yoga mat can give you this very discreet place and time to be asking yourself things like *what am I feeling here?* As a teacher I want to make space for what people are feeling. Sometimes I still don't know what I'm feeling right now. You want to start practicing and doing your poses with that type of experimentation and curiosity. Having that as my practice lab for now more than twenty years has infused it into every part of my life."

Anna goes on: "That definitely affected my experience of pregnancy, birth, and postpartum. My mindset would have been different without all the time I put into noticing sensation, and being more responsive to my body. For example, like most new parents, in the first few months after Hazel was born, I was exhausted, sleep deprived, not super tuned-in to my body, and just trying to keep everything going. But I would get these little glimpses where I knew certain things were happening in my body. I knew I needed to do some yoga or I'd not be a good person, or at least feeling good. With the experiences from my mat, I could sense this, notice it, and then respond to it. This is not something I could have done in the past. Not to make it sound easy—I go through stages of suppressing how I'm feeling, ignoring it, the ins and outs, just like everybody else."

With the help of movement, we become more aware of our body sensations and what our bodies need. Exercise represents an opportunity to give our bodies what they need. Too often, we only incorporate exercise into our lives in conjunction with a diet. Yet we do not have to be dieting to feel that same sense of self-efficacy in exercise. It feels good to respect and care for our bodies. Exercise is a practice where we can feel ourselves taking steps.

In another *Momma Bites!* interview, Angela Hawthorne, co-creator of Mind-Body Barre, shared her perspective on this relationship. "I think it's most important in terms of energy. Our energy becomes so stagnant. It's not about getting fit. It's important to move our bodies in ways where we can move energy to let go of that stagnant feeling. It's an important understanding in your body of when it's time to move and when it's time to sit still. If we're only doing one or the other, we're going to feel out of balance in many different areas of our lives."

Types of Exercise

Maybe Anna, Angela, or Courtney's stories have you ready to rock with exercise—but what to do? Our time is limited, so we want to do the 'right' kind of exercise. When I asked Dr. Davenport for her insight on this, she stated, "The research is not there yet around the type of exercise. We definitely see mental health benefits with yoga. Group exercise offers a combination of endorphin release, as well as socialization. We still do not know about the type of exercise that is most beneficial."

These ideas might sound exciting to some moms, while totally overwhelming to others. Too often, we conflate exercise with changes of clothes, and maximum aerobic effort. Dr. Davenport immediately smashes these myths. "When we talk about exercise, people usually picture people jogging, sweating, and out of breath. That's unappealing if you're not someone who likes to exercise at that level of intensity. But we find going for a nice walk is an excellent source of movement. It doesn't have to be in a thirty-minute bout. You can just park a little farther away from the grocery store. Get off the bus one stop early. Incorporating little bits of physical activity throughout your day has benefit. It doesn't have to be in a single twenty, thirty, or fifty minute chunk. It's also quite fine to do those higher intensity bouts if your body is ready to and you enjoy it. But understand intensity is not necessary to gain benefits."

Exercise: Types of Movement

List ways that you are already moving around throughout your days. There is no type of movement that does not count.

_____

_____

_____

_____

_____

What are some of the ways that you wish you could be more active?

_____

_____

_____

_____

_____

If not listed above, what are the most enjoyable or fun types of movement available to you right now?

_____

_____

_____

_____

_____

What is one type of movement that you could attempt (even just for ten minutes) sometime in the next few days?

_____

_____

_____

_____

_____

What type of support or equipment will you need to make this movement happen?

_____

_____

_____

_____

How can you commit to yourself to make this movement happen?

_____

_____

_____

_____

What sort of compassionate affirmations or reframes can you offer yourself if/when that movement does not go quite as you expect?

_____

_____

_____

_____

Who can you check in with to process your experience of this movement?

_____

_____

_____

_____

_____

There is no right or wrong type of movement for us. Dr. Davenport explains, "Most of the studies that are available on exercise in the postpartum period are actually based on walking. This really simple, low-cost activity has been associated with some pretty substantial improvements in depressive symptoms, cardiovascular health, and fitness. Find mom groups, connect with moms wishing to be active, grab your friends and family, and go for a walk. When I was in the postpartum period, I had just moved and did not have a lot of friends, so I would take my daughter for a walk nearly every day. It was a chance to bond together. It was also one of the only times that she would sleep, which was wonderful."

Signs of Readiness for Exercise

How do we know when we're ready to start exercising after having a baby? "Return to activity after delivery is really variable," Dr. Davenport advises. "With uncomplicated vaginal delivery, some women are able to begin some walking and light pelvic floor restorative exercises very soon, whereas women with complicated deliveries (episiotomies, cesarean sections) can take longer to heal."

When returning to exercise, make sure to listen to your body. Respect its signals. I could not wait to return to yoga after having my first baby. Not only did I want to have something just for me, I longed to move, and focus on offering some care to the body that carried, delivered, and fed my little one. As I neared the end of my first class, I noticed something new—back pain. Each class after, while I felt emotionally restored, my back hurt. "It's like my core is not strong enough or something," I told my teacher. "It's like I stretched too far or something." She asked some insightful questions, but was as puzzled as me. I kept coming back to this idea that I overstretched. It was an intuition that Dr. Andrea Wuotila confirmed years later in a *Momma Bites!* interview on chiropractic care (see Chapter 2 on page 23). "I see a lot of injuries leaping back into exercise. It's really important that you're safe about exercise, that you discuss your exercise routine with your midwife/OB, and listen to your body. There are some exercises (core work, for example) that we need to be thoughtful about. Even if you were super-fit before you gave birth, healing time is very important. A lot of women overlook how much laxity their body still has even after giving birth—especially if they breastfeed. We need to remain cautious as our joints have been compromised to some degree. We educate postpartum women about this. If you're noticing chronic aches and pains, you're probably doing too much and your body is probably not ready for it. Many of the women I see seem to have a timetable where six months out, they feel they should be entirely better. I remind them, it takes your body a year to get there, it's going to take at least a year (sometimes more) to get back. Sometimes these symptoms show up a year later—not necessarily right after having the baby. I dealt with some of these issues getting back into exercise too quickly. I was in that 'I've got to get my body back' zone, so I accumulated some injuries. I started working really soon after having both my girls and it wasn't the right thing for my body."

Signs you pushed it too hard:

- Bleeding restarts or worsens
- Sacroiliac (SI) joint pain
- Abdominal pain
- Chronic musculoskeletal issues (back pain, hip pain)

Support

It helps to find your people. The neighbor who walks her dog at the same time as I walk with my kids. The ladies at early morning classes. The yoga teacher who gives awesome assists. The other mom who walks her baby around the park. The barre teacher with the best playlist. The supportive social media group you can ask how to do a move. No mom is an island and we especially need sources of support to help motivate movement.

As a therapist who specializes in working with folks dealing with eating disorders, I am extremely picky about movement programs. Even a whisper of weight stigma or body shaming sends me in the opposite direction. The programs listed in the Resources section on page 229 are part of the movement revolution where brave leaders have pulled away from this damaging trope of the fitness industry. Let us follow their lead and find our way back into our amazing bodies.

> "Your body is not broken. Anything going wrong in your body is actually a part of your body seeking survival. We can easily look at that and say 'I'm falling apart, there's something wrong.' But the reality is, injuries are usually survival mechanisms. Your body's whole focus is to keep you going. When I'm feeling pain, instead of thinking *I'm falling apart,* flip it to *my body is working really hard to keep me going.* Nothing is broken. That's really important for a new mom, because often it feels like things really are broken."
>
> —Courtney Wyckoff, creator, Momma Strong

Notes

Blumenthal, James, Patrick Smith, and Benson Hoffman. "Is Exercise a Viable Treatment for Depression?" ACSM's Health & Fitness Journal, Volume 14, Issue 6, July 2012.

Guest-Jelley, Anna. "Curvy Yoga with Anna Guest-Jelley." Interview by Corinne Crossley, *Momma Bites! podcast,* March 2020.

Harvard Health Letter. "Exercise Is an All-Natural Treatment to Fight Depression." Harvard Medical School, April 2018. https://www.health .harvard.edu/mind-and-mood/exercise-is-an-all-natural-treatment -to-fight-depression

Harvard Medical School. "How Does Exercise Help Us Relax?" Harvard Health Publishing, July 13, 2018. https://www.health.harvard.edu/staying -healthy/exercising-to-relax

Hawthorne, Angela. "Changing Your Relationship with Exercise." Interview by Corinne Crossley, *Momma Bites! podcast,* February 2020.

Mayo Clinic, "Biofeedback." Last accessed December 19, 2019. https://www .mayoclinic.org/tests-procedures/biofeedback/about/pac-20384664

Platt, Marc, and Ric Kidney. *Legally Blond.* Metro-Goldwyn-Mayer. July 13, 2001.

Wuotila, Andrea. "Postpartum Chiropractic Care." Interview by Corinne Crossley, *Momma Bites! podcast,* February 2020.

Wyckoff, Courtney. "Courtney Wyckoff: Mother of Momma Strong." Interview by Corinne Crossley and Jessica Foley, *Momma Bites! podcast,* November 12, 2018.

Chapter 9:
Getting Reacquainted
Body Image

"Ugh, I know I'm not supposed to, but I *really* want to go on a diet," Dahlia says, wincing. Since I am clear about my non-diet approach to eating disorders recovery, I know she's nervous to say this to me. I nod, sympathetically. While she may be surprised, I'd been anticipating this for a while. Dahlia is six months postpartum with a lifelong history of dieting and body hatred. "I nursed her for four months and that was a misery. All that weight loss that was supposed to happen with nursing—I didn't see it! I think it's time that I do something about this."

"What needs to be done?"

"I've got to lose this weight! I want my body back!"

"Back to what?" I ask.

"To how it was before I had my baby."

"There's no such thing as having your 'pre-baby' body back," I say, emphasizing with air quotes. "Dahlia, you were in therapy with me for a year before you even got pregnant. There was not one session that you felt remotely satisfied or even neutral about your body."

She laughs. "I know. And now I'd kill to have that body back."

"Right. And how often in your life have you done this cycle—despising your body, or at least being dissatisfied with it, only to look back on it and desperately wish you could have that body again?"

She sighs. "Like, my whole life."

"Right. So, what makes now different?"

"I don't know! Doesn't everyone diet after they have the baby? Isn't that part of being a new mom? Doesn't everyone want their pre-baby body back?"

Sigh. Okay, let's start off with a couple of things here. I see this a lot. Working with people with eating disorders, I counsel a number of mothers in recovery or struggling with recovery throughout their pregnancy. In many cases throughout pregnancy and after, I see women finally able to get into recovery.

At the same time, I find when moms hit the six-month mark (sometimes earlier, sometimes later) something changes for them. They've settled into a more adjusted life with their baby, no longer a newborn. Mom has something resembling a routine. There is a rhythm to nursing, pumping, and eating. Maybe the baby has a "bedtime" or certain number of hours they sleep for a stretch. No more scuba diving. Less fumbling. Less of a beginner-mom's mind. Predictably, the focus turns back to them. Compassion no longer feels like an urgent necessity. These moms believe they should have things together. "After all, it's been six (or whatever number) months!" When I invite them to consider that this length of time is simultaneously both a lifetime, and not very long at all, they scoff. The rush to get back to "pre-baby body" keeps them from curiosity about their postpartum body, opting instead for muscling it to where it started.

Diets and Pre-Baby Body Bullsh!t

Ugh, the "pre-baby body" myth. The latest development in crushing standards of female beauty. Only for a medical condition exclusively associated with women would society assume a rapid return to our pre-condition state. I suppose we should feel fortunate that bookstores do not feature titles like *Get Back to Your Pre-Ovarian Cancer Weight!* or *Lose Those Pesky Breast Cancer Pounds.* Nope, it's only those exclusively female transitions (namely pregnancy and menopause) that are synonymous with expectations of time traveling our bodies.

Guess what? There is no such thing as getting back to your pre-baby body. No matter what happens, your body will never *not* have had a baby. Thank goodness. Our bodies gave us the greatest possible gift. Despite our judgments of it, this body carried a baby. It shall never be pre-baby again.

Yet, the drumbeat continues. Our exposure to headlines like "Back to Her Pre-Baby Body in Just One Month!" used to be limited to supermarket checkouts. Now with every type of online media tailored to our interests, we are bombarded. Stories pop up in our Instagram feeds, as ads attached to articles, clickbait in every new browser window—algorithms conflating our postpartum interests (with curiosity about how fast a Kardashian loses her baby weight).

Media fed us (pun intended) this line for over a hundred years. Unrealistic beauty standards are lucrative money-making outlets. In 2016, according to Orbis market research, the weight-loss and diet industry accounted for $169 billion with expectations to grow to $279 billion by 2023. Our body dissatisfaction is worth a lot of money. It sells two major things—media and diets. If you've never thought about it before, take a second to consider the industry behind the perfect images of perfect bodies. Sarah Coyne, PhD, and Toni Liechty, PhD, shared their compelling research on the effect of media on pregnant and postpartum women when I invited them on the *Momma Bites!* podcast. One of their studies examined effects of print media images on pregnant and postpartum women. Sarah explains, "Women brought into the laboratory were asked to read a magazine that was similar across all conditions, except for one page. The one different page had a typical celebrity magazine's article featuring gorgeous pregnant women or an article with a headline 'My Body after Pregnancy, How I Lost All the Weight,' with the celebrity looking fabulous in a bikini. In the other condition, there was an article about decorating with fruit—something not body-related at all. We found that even after just five minutes of looking at the magazine, our pregnant participants reported feeling worse about their bodies than those who had read the fruit-decorating version. That was pretty powerful to me. I thought, *Five minutes, that's all it takes to knock women down in terms of how they feel about their bodies after looking at these images.*"

One page in a whole magazine. Five minutes. That's all they needed to change how these women felt about their bodies. Learning to be critical media consumers is a necessary part of our body image self-care plan. Consuming these images increases risks of depression and body dissatisfaction. Who has the mental energy to fight off diet culture and perfectionistic body standards when we have babies to care for? We need to take better care of ourselves than that.

Tips for critical media consumption:
- Tread carefully with magazines, television shows, and social media influencers whose chief message is focused around appearances. As

you have just read, even short exposures to this material promote negative body image.

- Pay attention to your thoughts and feelings as you consume media. How do you feel about yourself while consuming or after consuming any given type of media? If reading an article about a particular type of wallpaper makes you feel bad about yourself, stop reading it! Trust yourself and respect your own reactions.

- Periodically remind yourself of the filtering and retouching of images. No matter how aware we are of this process, it is still jarring to see videos of this process. The most widely known and acclaimed example of this is the Dove Evolution video done for the Dove campaign for real beauty.

Weight loss is not required to pursue positive states (health, positive self esteem, sexuality, happiness). Most of my clients who have lost weight found their emotional expectations for a given weight to be incorrect. Every SlimFast and Weight Watchers commercial shows us happy, confident "success" stories. Every keto and paleo blog professes clear-mindedness. With that brainwashing, of course we'd expect arrival into a smaller body to solve everything. But it doesn't.

We believe dieting will quell food obsession, yet it often worsens it. My clients report when they were closing in on their "ideal" weight that they were more obsessed with food and weight than ever. Clients who participated in Weight Watchers found when they were closest to their lifetime membership weight (the idealized weight at which the company waives their membership fee as long as participants stay within two pounds) they felt most miserable and food/weight-obsessed. It was the opposite of their prediction. They could not have imagined a situation where they weighed the "right" number but still felt miserable. How could they have? Everyone told them this weight would bring happiness and health—not obsession and misery.

Dieting as Self-Care?

"I just can't figure out why I can't stay on a diet," Heather announces, sitting down to session.

"What happens?" I ask.

"I do amazing for a certain period of time. I am a champion dieter. When I'm on, I'm on. I prep all my meals, count all my points/calories/carbs/macros, whatever I'm doing. I look at menus online if I'm going out to dinner later and then plan my eating around that meal. I go to sleep earlier because I don't want to be tempted to eat at night. Since I'm in bed earlier, it's easier to get up and exercise before the kids get up or before I have to go to work. When I'm on, I'm on."

"And when you're not . . . "

"I grab anything I can, whenever I can. I eat the kids' leftover breakfast either as my breakfast or in addition to my breakfast. I never pack my lunch or have snacks with me, so I end up going to the vending machine or getting something at Starbucks with my afternoon coffee. I need coffee because I stay up late watching shows, especially if I've eaten something after dinner because I don't want to go to bed after I've eaten something. When I'm up late, I'm exhausted in the morning, so it's tough to get out of bed for work, and impossible to exercise before the kids are up. I feel gross all the time. If I could just stay on a diet, I would feel so much better."

While I've had this interaction with many clients over the years, this time I recall distinctly. In the years of practicing psychotherapy before having kids, I counseled several moms with eating disorders, body image disturbance, and chronic dieting behaviors. Heather was one of my typically smart, high-achieving, hard-charging, ever-providing moms. It was not until this discussion that I realized dieting is a socially acceptable way moms pursue self-care. What a lightbulb moment! I had not put it together until then. Hearing the complete disparity between the care, planning, and concern she offered herself when she was on a diet, contrasted with the complete disregard she had for her own needs when she was not, finally drove the point home.

"What would it be like to do these things for yourself—meal prep, pack lunches, accessible snacks, balancing your needs throughout the day, without being on a diet?"

"Ugh! What's the point? Who has the time? Just tonight, my oldest has soccer, the three-year-old has dance, and I have to run to the store because the baby is out of food pouches."

"But you'd make time if you're on a diet."

"Yes."

"What's so different about being on a diet?"

Diets by the Numbers

So, what *is* so different about being on a diet? Diets allure us with their clear, "simple" plans. For a price, food shows up to our door, one major decision off our proverbial plates. Diets organize the chaos around how to spend our time, money, and attention. Diets say, "Don't worry about this, mama, I got it—I'll tell you what to eat, I'll make you stay the course, and prioritize getting the food you're supposed to have." And diets offer hope. The illusion that an oasis of ease is coming with a smaller body.

Until we become the 98 percent. What 98 percent? The 98 percent of diets that fail. You read that right. Of the millions of people dieting today, within five years, they will have gained it back. All of it. And in many cases, more. When your existence has been dieting, restricting, and hating on your body until it is the right size, re-gain feels horrific. Failure. Like being forced to live in bodies that have given up on us. Walking around in bodies that evidence our failings.

Can you imagine any other medical intervention with a 98 percent failure rate? If you went to your doctor for an uncomfortable, chronic rash and she said "I'm writing you a prescription for a topical ointment. It works amazing for six months. You'll feel amazing, and get recognition from other people about how great your skin looks. After the six months are up though, 98 percent of the people who use this lotion report the rash returns, and is often worse than before. Also, it's common to feel really depressed after the rash comes back, and you will blame yourself (not the medication) when it returns. What pharmacy should I send this to?"

Do you pick up that prescription, or do you ask if there's another way?

Diet Culture

What do I mean "diet culture?" Diet culture is more than just a restrictive eating plan for weight loss (that's a diet). Diet culture comprises messages that idealize thin, attractive, as well as white, young, and able bodies. These ideals are considered to be the standards of beauty in our culture. Deviations from these standards are deemed unattractive and unhealthy—conditions that need intervention. This is especially troubling because so few of us ever hit the genetic lottery these standards demand. Diet culture is inextricably connected to beauty culture. Even when we are not labeled as too fat by diet culture, our societal obsession with having the "right" kind of body tells us to scrub off blemishes, keep away wrinkles, straighten/soften our hair, and whatever we do, be pretty.

Even worse than beauty standards are the ways diet culture defines health. Physical health is the mighty sword that diet culture wields to keep us stuck. How many times have you heard "but I have to lose the weight to be healthy?" Countless. We say this to ourselves. We say this to each other. We say this about our loved ones. It is a terribly damaging myth. You read that right—it is a myth.

Health at Every Size (Yes, Even the One You Are Right Now)

Over a decade ago, a major shift happened in the field of eating disorders when Linda Bacon published her groundbreaking book *Health at Every Size: The Surprising Truth about Your Weight*. While revolutionary to our diet-obsessed culture, the book's tenets were simple and common sense. A psychotherapist, researcher, and recovered dieter, Bacon dedicated her career to understanding the interplay of weight, health, and weight stigma.

Here are some of those key tenets adapted for the postpartum perspective:

- Weight is a poor indicator of health. When we use weight as a metric, vast numbers of people are over-tested (people in large bodies) and under-tested (people in small bodies).
- Many of the conditions associated with overweight (heart disease, diabetes) are best treated with increased movement, rather than weight loss.
- You do not have to be a certain size to pursue health. Health is not a number on a scale. Health is a collection of behaviors. Exercise, sleep hygiene, gentle non-restrictive nutrition, and other foundational self-care are behaviors that embody health. You do not have to wait until you are a certain number on a scale to pursue health. You can start this very second.
- All bodies are good bodies. There is no wrong way to have a body. It is our misplaced standards of beauty that are wrong. Our stigmatization of people in large bodies needs to stop. Our bodies are not the problem.
- Bodies, especially postpartum bodies, do not need fixing. Some need more time to heal, but there is nothing to fix. Bodies need care. They just do.

The Health at Every Size (HAES) approach offers an entirely different perspective than the dominant cultural narrative, yet it makes so much more sense. When yo-yo dieting is scientifically linked with risks for diabetes and heart disease, the clear answer is not another diet, but rather to take care of our bodies as kindly as we care for everyone else.

Still having trouble with this idea? Try this brainteaser I present my clients. Imagine a meteor hit the Earth and the only effect it had on humanity was that you could never change your weight. No matter what you do, you can neither lose nor gain weight. Everything else is the same. Your responsibilities, energy requirements, and physical experience of nutrition and movement remain the same. How would you take care of your body?

Think about it.

Sometimes clients respond with their inner ten-year-old. "Are you kidding me? I would eat nothing but junk food, never work out," etc. But I remind them of the catch. You still have to live your life. You still need to feel well enough to move through the world—with kids. You need energy, strength, and resilience. Usually people reconsider their answer at that point.

How about you? What ways are you putting off taking care of yourself because your body is not the right size? Are you eating foods you hate in hopes that you'll lose weight? Are you madly working out in your home when what you crave is a Zumba class? What is it that you're neglecting because your body is not the right size?

Body Image

You may be thinking *big surprise, dieting sucks and is soul crushing—how do I actually improve my postpartum body image?* Let's back up for a sec and define what we're talking about. I went to look up body image in some very fancy and reputable dictionaries and hated all of the definitions. So, here's my definition. Body image is an individual's spectrum of emotions about their physical appearance and abilities. Body image can be highly influenced by cultural factors, external messages, environmental factors, and upbringing. Listed below are some things that contribute to one's body image experience throughout development and daily life:

- **Early media consumption:** what you watched, read, and absorbed as a kid via television, movies, magazines, and other media.
- **Early family messages:** How were bodies talked about in your family? How was your body spoken about? How about your mother's? Other female relatives?
- **Early friend messages:** Did any of your childhood friends criticize their body, your body, or other people's bodies? Were you ever bullied for your body?

- **Sports/body-based activities (includes dance):** How effective did your body feel in your participation? Did you participate in sports where it was preferable to be a certain size or shape?
- **Diets:** What age was your first diet? How many diets have you tried?
- **Eating disorders:** Do you or anyone in your family have a history of or current eating disorder? People in your immediate circle with an active eating disorder? Have you seen anyone recover? Lifelong struggles?
- **Body talkers (yours):** How do the people in your life talk about your body (if they do)? Include inferences and indirect communication.
- **Body talkers (theirs):** How do the people closest in your life talk about their bodies? How do they speak about others' bodies (including celebrities)?
- **Past experience of significant weight gains or losses:** How many times have you experienced significant weight gains or losses where your body shape changed quickly? This may or may not include dieting, puberty, inadvertent losses/gains.
- **Current media consumption:** What forms of media do you consume? How much of this programming focuses on appearances?
- **Influencers:** What type of social media influencers do you follow? What is the focus of their message? What products are they selling?
- **Fitness industry:** What messages are at the forefront of the fitness trends you follow? What do the instructors look like?

Consider how these different elements affected and still influence your body image. Understanding the full scope of how our body image is constructed provides tools to improve it.

Believe it or not, we do not start feeling better about our bodies by changing the way they look. We start feeling better about our bodies by changing the way we care for them. For some moms, being confident in a postpartum body feels overwhelming. Remember, this is about improving body image.

Improvement takes time and happens in stages. As a clinician, I am hugely grateful for the body positive movement. It is a life-changer for so many and an integral part of their recovery. At the same time, many people feel daunted by the prospect of feeling positive about their body. Body positivity feels like a different planet from where they live.

Marci Evans, registered dietitian and self-described food and body image healer, echoed this experience in her work. In our *Momma Bites!* podcast interview she shared her work with clients who felt shut-down by the term "body positive." "I focus on healing body image. Healing looks different for different people. Each of us has a body narrative formed by our life experiences, different identities, family dynamics, and the larger culture. All this creates our own unique body image story that we hold inside ourselves. That story is how we experience our body image. As we begin to look at that body image story, it creates opportunities to introduce kindness, compassion, or self-understanding. Even just acknowledging *Wow, my body has been through a lot, holds a lot, and does a lot*, can be part of the healing process."

At the center of her work, Marci reframes the concept of body image into a relationship. She continues, "Body image is something with which we have a relationship. When working with clients dealing with negative body image, it's about being able to renegotiate the relationship so that it feels less fraught, consuming—so there is a little more ease. The way that I conceptualize this relationship repair is to compare it to therapy. When we go to therapy, we don't have the goal of only feeling happy in therapy. There are days when we feel more positive about our body image, days when we feel neutral, and days when we feel really negatively about our bodies. The idea is cultivating a relationship where we move through these moods with less pain and more self-compassion."

Improving our relationship with our body image is not all-or-nothing. There is no finish line. When cultivating more positive body esteem (positive or compassionate feelings toward our bodies), any movement toward increased appreciation is progress. As Marci explained, this is about cultivating skills to take care of our body image, especially when it needs attention. It is about noticing the wish to diet and seeing that as a sign of depletion rather than the need to start restricting.

Working on improving our body image recruits those same skills of curiosity discussed throughout this book. Even if we are not happy with our appearance, many moms can consider ways our body showed up for us this year. This curiosity is an excellent foundation for cultivating appreciation for our bodies, even if more in function. Think of curiosity and appreciation as a set of muscles you want to strengthen. Body image does not improve if we do not work those muscles. Contrary to what diet culture tells us, positive body image does not come upon us instantly like an "after" photo. Rather, it is comprised of stringing together neutral-to-positive events and beliefs about your body, one after another, like pearls on a string. At first, collecting these pearls can be difficult and slow-going. They may feel microscopic or insignificant. But eventually, the more we practice this, the more savvy we get at finding them.

Anna's Story

Anna Guest-Jelley is the creator of Curvy Yoga, author and (at the time of our interview) mom to a nine-month-old. As she is a body-positive advocate in the public eye, I deeply appreciated her authenticity discussing her journey with body positivity.

She says: "When I was growing up, from a very young age—five or earlier—my pediatrician told my mom I was too far on the growth chart and I should lose weight. My mom, like many people, had her own lifetime of dieting and food issues (as did pretty much every woman in my family). She was all too ripe for that conversation. That started me down a path of many different diets. I did some calorie restriction before my first official diet (Weight Watchers) when I was around ten years old. This continued until my late twenties, until finally one day I tallied up that I had been on sixty-five different diets. When I saw that number, it was such a stark moment I don't think I'll ever forget. I realized if sixty-five diets had not "worked," the answer probably did not lie in the sixty-sixth. I needed a whole different approach to my body. However, since I had done all these diets, I had no connection to my body. I had outsourced everything about hunger. I had no sense of what hunger was. All of that was from a piece of paper that said 'here's what you eat, here's how you exercise.'

"Now that I've been doing Curvy Yoga for over ten years, people assume that body acceptance comes easily to me. But it's still a process. It's not like I just snapped my fingers, accepted my body, and then that was the end. That's how I thought it would be at first. That's one of the things I love about yoga as a tool for body acceptance, because yoga gives us a framework of practice. Body acceptance is a lifelong practice. It's not as if I will never have a negative thought about my body again; of course I will. I've had those thoughts drilled into me. But I can see how different it is in my relationship with my body right now. Now when stuff pops up for me, it's an invitation to pause and ask myself *I wonder why I feel like throwing all my clothes out and burning them? I wonder why I'm being negative about my body?* I'm usually stressed or anxious about something else entirely. I have a habit of displacing that onto my body, and now that I can see that it, it makes a huge difference."

Remember, for those moms struggling in the darkest of places with their bodies, there is still hope. The bridge from hatred to positivity is not love—it is curiosity. Love is too tall an order for those stuck in pervasively negative body image. Do not focus on positivity. Learn to stoke curiosity.

Be gentle and remind yourself, the construction of anything positive cannot be built with cruelty or negativity. At times, you might get incredibly frustrated with yourself. We may rail on a particularly difficult day, thinking *Why am I still struggling with body image after all this time?* I include myself in this. In more insightful moments, I have to laugh at myself and my instinct toward self-criticism. *This is not something you can bully yourself into,* I remind myself. Struggle is a sign that you need more compassion, not less.

More Roads to Improving Body Image

The problem with body image issues is that we get stuck in the image part. We get so focused on how we look, we stop being present with living our lives. Contrary to what we are taught by society, our bodies are instruments, not objects. Our heads are for protecting our brains, not vehicles for perfect hair. Our faces are meant to express feelings and to connect with our babies, not a canvas for make-up. And so on. As a society, we are increasingly out-of-step with what our bodies can do and more focused on how they look. A major shift in improving body image comes from focusing on function of one's body over appearance.

One caveat for this next exercise, which focuses on body function—not everyone's body works in the same ways—especially since having a baby. Challenges with functional abilities are a factor in body image. All of the parts listed may not work perfectly, but I believe at least some of the parts on this list still support your ability and movement through the world.

Exercise: What's Your Purpose?

Jot down some notes about the function of each of these body parts. What they look like is immaterial.

Eyes: _____

_____

_____

Nose: _____

_____

_____

Mouth: _____

_____

_____

Face: _____

_____

_____

Neck: _____

_____

_____

Back: _____

_____

_____

Stomach: _____

_____

_____

Breasts: _____

_____

_____

Butt: _____

_____

_____

Legs: _____

_____

_____

Arms: _____

_____

_____

Feet: _____

_____

_____

Use and Move Your Body

"Ugh, I hate the gym," Molly says, cringing in one of our initial therapy sessions, "but I know I should go."

"What made you think of the gym?" I ask.

"You asked what I was doing for exercise?"

"I asked how you enjoyed moving your body."

"Same thing," she dismisses.

"Nope. Gyms are buildings. Movement or exercise are activities. You can hate the gym, but most everyone enjoys some sort of movement. A walk on the beach, playing in a pool, yard work—it all counts."

"Oh, then that is different. Well, I really enjoy dancing with Esme," she says, referring to her eleven-month-old. "She giggles like crazy and I find myself dancing around the kitchen like a nut. I hold her or sometimes we get going so much, I put her in her high chair and dance to entertain her. Actually, I get pretty sweaty doing that."

"But you weren't counting that as movement?"

"No."

"Why?"

"No sports bra, no plan, it only lasts a few songs."

"But you love it."

"Yes."

"And when you're having a mommy-daughter dance party, what are you focused on? How your body looks or how it feels to move?"

"Dancing. Moving. Making her laugh."

"We can build on that."

Our bodies are meant for use. Modern dance, tai chi, parkour—humans have created an incredible array of activities for using our bodies. "Your body doesn't exist just to be viewed as an aesthetic object. It also allows you to function in the world. For women who have been pregnant, it allowed you to create a whole human person—that's a huge thing to focus on. I think a lot of times we shift too far toward prioritizing appearance when there are so many other elements that matter when it comes to your body—especially during this life stage," Dr. Toni Liechty, PhD, discussed. Focusing on appearance often shuts down our participation in fun activities. Conversely, when we get into the flow of things we love, the negative voices in our heads go quiet (or quieter).

Ways to use your body:

- **Move your body and tune into its strength.** Doing things that make you feel strong helps improve your body image. Whether lifting weights, turning over soil in a garden, or swinging a portable car seat to entertain your baby, move your body and tune into its strength.

- **When you have the energy, do something with your body that feels productive.** Plant a flower, scrub something, or paint a wall (not a whole room). Connect to the ways your entire body makes this happen. Paint does not get on the wall without your entire body working toward that goal.

- **Even just for five or ten minutes, do the projects that you set aside after your baby was born.** Projects are a beautiful way to live in your body. Knitting, sketching, embroidery, calligraphy, collaging—whatever you love, find your flow. Too many people put aside artistic or creative endeavors feeling that any spare time should be employed in pursuit of exercise or weight-loss methods. Connect with your body and its abilities as you live in it now. Knit a row or two. Paint a jewelry box. Collage an ornament. Keep it small and achievable. In our interview on body image, Dr. Sarah Coyne, PhD, professor and researcher, shared her experience of healing her own body image in this way. "In the postpartum period, remember to focus on your talents and seeing yourself as a whole individual—not necessarily what you look like. Last year, my eleven-year-old daughter asked me to try out for community theater with her. It was terrifying, but when your eleven-year-old wants to do something with you, you say yes. We went up there on stage and we're singing and dancing, and it actually ended up being so beautifully healing of my body image issues. I had just had my fifth child, which is a lot of kids and a lot of changes to your body. It was so powerful to do something with my body and develop my talents around that. It was really healing for me. It was really scary, but it was great."

- **If a bigger project feels too overwhelming, tackle a household chore with awareness.** While doing dishes, folding laundry, or even changing your baby, think about all these movements that are required of your body.

- **Think of experiences you would love and figure out a way to make them happen, even if on a smaller scale.** Bodies are vehicles for experiences. Our bodies are meant to carry us through nature walks, do our bidding at bowling, or walk through an art museum. Bowl for fun and skill enhancement. Try out your baby carrier on a flat, short nature trail. Look around for a smaller-sized museum or gallery to explore.

Self-Care with Clothes

"Ugh," Maria says, pulling at her top in our afternoon session, "this bra sucks."

"Oh, man, pokey underwire? Those are the worst!" I empathize.

"No, zero support. They were great for nursing, but it's like wearing an old sock now."

"Wait, that's a nursing bra?" I respond, incredulous. "How long has it been since you nursed?"

She smiles sheepishly. "Six months."

"Do you have any new bras since you stopped nursing?"

"No, I've been living in them forever. Worse still, these are the ones from when I nursed my four-year-old."

"Why not get new bras?"

"I don't know. I guess I was waiting until my body settled after nursing. I had no idea what size I would end up being."

"Understood, but it's been six months since you finished weaning. Would you say that you've probably settled on a size?"

"Probably. I wanted it to be a smaller one."

"Okay, but think of how each tug and adjustment silently reminds you of your discomfort. Those breasts fed your sons for how long?"

"Combined . . . " she calculates in her head, "twenty-five months."

"Twenty-five! Is that how you treat the employees that fed your babies for two straight years?"

She laughs.

"I'm serious! You wouldn't treat a childcare provider that way. You'd express gratitude and make sure they felt supported and appreciated."

"I would," she agrees, laughing more.

"Frankly, those girls deserve better."

Maria took our conversation seriously. In the weeks after this session, she took a few hours and went shopping for some clothes, especially bras. She came in delighted with how much better she felt. She had not noticed the subtle messages her ill-fitting clothes sent to her overall sense of well-being and body esteem.

This is why fit is so important. Moms want to hold off until they are at the "right" size before they go shopping. "I don't want to waste the money," clients tell me, "especially since we have less money with me on maternity leave." I get it. But ill-fitting clothes are a constant reminder that your body is a size that does not deserve new clothes. Getting some new (or new to you) clothes is a gesture of acceptance and appreciation to your postpartum body.

Tips for shopping for your postpartum body:

- Go when you have time. This is not a process to rush.
- Use the changing rooms for more than nursing. Take your time considering how things fit and feel. Stand, sit, crouch, bend over in whatever you're purchasing.
- If the lighting in the changing rooms sucks, take the garments home. I adore Target to the depths of my soul, though I wonder who on Earth looks good in their dressing room lighting.
- If you are breastfeeding, nursing tops have come a long way but can be expensive sometimes. A button-down top or flowy top that can be easily lifted works just as well.
- Consider the texture and weight of the fabric. Body temperatures fluctuate wildly postpartum. Anything too light could have you shivering, while a big, chunky sweater could leave you trapped in a woolen prison.
- **Do Not** buy an aspirational size. This is about buying clothes that fit *today*. Aspirational clothes do not work. Would you put your baby in a onesie a size or two too small?
- Clear out your closet of the sizes that no longer fit (or at least put them away for a while).
- Consider giving your "give-ups" a break for a while. Give-ups are those parts of your wardrobe that say "f*ck off, the only thing that matters

to me is comfort." Dressing for the requirements of the job of motherhood is foremost, but if you find yourself in the same sweatshirt every day, or the thought anything other than your daily yoga pants puts you into a fear sweat, it is time to check in with yourself. Beyond comfy, how does wearing these clothes make you feel about your body?

- The size of everything changes in pregnancy and postpartum. Do not forget to pick up some shoes.

Plan for Pitfalls

The road toward positive body image is not necessarily a straight one. We all have setbacks. The idea is not to prevent setbacks, but rather to have skills to recover from them. Below are a few common triggers for setbacks.

Loss of Control

No matter how universal to parenting, lack of control is a tough pill to swallow. This issue arose in my conversation with Marci Evans. "Often a theme of becoming a parent is the ways we can feel out of control. When we are pregnant, our bodies can feel out of control. The labor and delivery process can feel out of control. As our children get older and develop a larger sense of self, independence, and autonomy (which we want), we realize on a different level, this child is their own person. Body image becomes this handy container to hold all those deeper, complicated feelings we tuck away inside of ourselves. It happens unconsciously—we find ourselves more preoccupied with what we are eating, what our stomach looks like, whether we have exercised today, or that our lunch became the scraps of kid leftovers. These experiences can be a conduit to work out those complicated feelings. We attempt to manage those loss-of-control feelings by trying to control our bodies."

It is well established in the field of eating disorders that disordered behaviors develop from the wish to manage stressful events or situations in the lives of sufferers. Even if you do not consider yourself or any of your behaviors on the eating disorder spectrum, usually the metaphor still applies. "Things would be so much better if I just lost weight," or "I know it wouldn't fix everything, but being thinner would just make my life easier," or "I can't control all this craziness in my life, but I can control what I put in my mouth" are all fruits of this same tree. Even knowing this, the impulse can still feel so real. This is not isolated to parenting-related issues—dealing with a stressful boss, managing care of a sick loved one, or ferrying through transition. Alongside these significant stressors, we find ourselves frustrated by our bodies, wishing to change them.

If you notice this experience, be curious about it.
- When did you notice the increase in these thoughts?
- What are the situations in which you feel most out of control?
- Which feels more within your control—your body, or the stressful event?

The idea here is not to argue with your mind, but to become practiced at noticing when you're feeling triggered, and implementing other skills to manage it.

Marci shared her own experience wrestling with this issue with her son's premature birth. "There were so many difficult moments and so many unknowns. There were times where I felt like I had no control. There were moments where I actually had no control over what was happening. One of the most helpful tools I practiced (from the work I do with clients) was bringing myself back to the present moment. I'm really great at playing the "what if" game and creating scary scenarios in my head. So often through that difficult time, I practiced saying to myself *Just be right here. Right here, right now is where your power is.* Or *I can do this moment and that's all I have to do.*"

Media and Social Media

Media bombards every day. Print and broadcast media used to determine the entirety of the media messaging in our lives. Now social media infiltrates our lives more than ever before. In our interview on media and body image, Dr. Sarah Coyne, PhD, shared how media captured even her in a postpartum vulnerability. "I've researched media's impact on children and families for the last couple of decades, especially getting into the body image research area once I had a daughter. During the early postpartum phase after my third child, I was really into the show *America's Next Top Model*. I'd watch it and notice I'd feel really bad about myself. I thought, isn't that interesting? I began wondering about the impact media had on the way postpartum women felt about their bodies. It was a different age group than I had ever studied before. It's a really vulnerable time of life and there is hardly any research on it in terms of body image." From this experience, Sarah innovated several studies cited in this chapter. If a brilliant researcher like Sarah can get snared by media's assault on body image, no one is immune.

When possible, consider tailoring your media diet, especially your social media diet, to sources that support your body esteem. "There's research to show how different social media platforms tend to influence body image," Dr. Coyne cites. "Image-based social media platforms like Instagram tend to have the greatest effect on women. There is even research to suggest attaching disclaimers like 'this is photoshopped' still results in women feeling bad about themselves after seeing those types of photos. Women must be good critical consumers of media, as media has such a powerful impact on the way that we think about ourselves."

Instagram and Facebook are simultaneously rife with triggers, but also goldmines for anti-diet, body positive, size diversity connections as well. "One of the key issues is how the message is presented," Dr. Liechty emphasized. "There's research that shows even messages designed to inspire exercise (fitsporation/fitspo), when appearance-based, have a negative impact on women's body image. It doesn't motivate them. Whereas if it's more honest and focused on health outcomes, feeling good, or accepting your body, then it has a positive impact. There are a lot of complexities in the nuance of the message, and making sure that it's not just focused on exclusively appearance is important."

Dr. Coyne continues, "It's really hard to know, especially with the speed at which we filter through media. If you're scrolling through Instagram, you're probably not taking a lot of time to critically reflect on each image. The best litmus test is whether it elicits self-criticism. Ask yourself *when I look at this, does it make me feel bad about myself?* If an image makes us feel bad about our bodies, it has a negative impact. A lot of people think *if I don't like the way I look, it will motivate me to be more active, eat better, etc.* But the research shows that's not what happens. The worse we feel about our bodies, the more likely we are to have heightened depression, the more likely we are to overeat, the less likely we are to be active because we feel bad. It makes some logical sense. If we view certain media and it makes us criticize our bodies, that's media we should avoid." Curate your social media to eliminate those exposures that make you feel bad about yourself and boost those who help you feel empowered, accepting, and embodied.

Comparison Minds

"Look at this newborn portrait. What a perfect little sleeping baby!" "How has she lost all her baby weight already?" "Oh my God, their holiday decorations are up so early, and look totally amazing!" Sound familiar? Humans are judgmental beings. Evolution selected those who were quickest to judgment, as we were the ones who survived longest. While judgment kept us going as a species, it messes with us on an individual level with comparisons. Notice when you find your head stuck in comparisons. Step back. Be curious about what it is that this person or situation brings up for you. Remind yourself that you do not know the whole truth of this person's life or experience. I promise you, everyone (yes, everyone) feels they come up short in one way or another.

Dr. Coyne provides an intervention for managing our comparison minds. "There's some really interesting research that says, if you're looking at a picture and realizing you're comparing yourself to someone, stop and wonder *What's this person's story? What makes her cry in the middle of the night?*

What are her fears? Her traumas? What are the things she really struggles with? What you're doing in that process is humanizing rather than objectifying that individual. When you humanize people, we compare ourselves less to them. It's an effective strategy to consider someone's wider story, rather than just the filtered image they decided to post on Instagram that day."

Meditation for Body Image

I know, the last thing a new mom feels she has is space to meditate. But you had to expect meditation somewhere in a book on self-care. One of my favorite forms of meditation is a Metta, or lovingkindness meditation. Who couldn't use some of that?

Exercise: Metta Meditation

Read the following statements and repeat them to yourself. Imagine offering these as wishes for a beloved friend or family member. Take all the time you need as you move through each phrase, offering it authentically.

May you feel loved.

May you breathe easy.

May you feel strong.

May you feel free of tension.

May you feel joy.

May you be free of pain.

May you feel energetic.

May you rest easy.

May you be nourished.

May you be appreciated.

May you be loved.

Repeat the meditation, next offering these wishes for someone you do not know very well or do not know personally. If you feel stuck on who to imagine offering these phrases, consider offering all bodies of the world these wishes. Again, offer these phrases as authentically as possible.

Finally, repeat the meditation, offering these wishes to yourself and your body. Offer them authentically. Draw on those skills or experiences of offering these phrases to others, even all those on the Earth (remember, this includes you).

Support

Attending to our relationship with our body image is a major element of self-care. Some days, that may feel effortless. We feel present in our bodies. We can thank them silently for their abilities to heal, hold babies, and run the motherhood marathon. Other days, we feel fractured and disembodied. We have the urge to punish our bodies for not following our bidding. We feel angry at ourselves for inadequate efforts at making our bodies look how they should. It is these days that we need support.

For many of us, our first instinct for support may be to look to our friends and family. If we have great, supportive people around us, this is an excellent intervention. Reach out. Let people know you are struggling with your body image. Resist the urge to get into the litany of things you hate about your body today. Rather, let your loved one know "I'm having a bad body image day." Getting into a debate of how great or not great you look is not helpful. Having a vent session about how much you and your support person both hate your bodies is especially unhelpful. If those around you can't support you without getting snared in ripping on their body, they are not a helpful support person, even if they have the best of intentions. Finding a place of comfort and connection without these types of collusion is a real source of support.

Remember, your body image struggles might take others by surprise. The obvious flaws in our bodies usually aren't to others. A particularly poignant example of this dynamic came up in my interview with Drs. Liechty and Coyne. They are actually longtime childhood friends. Dr. Liechty disclosed, "I remember the first time Sarah told me as a friend that she was having some concerns about body image. I think I probably laughed and said, 'What? That's not possible, you look great!' My first reaction was, 'When I look at you, you look great, therefore it never occurred to me that you might be having body image concerns.' I think we have to remember when we're supporting our friends and loved ones that you can't see body image concerns from the outside. You may think someone looks great and can't understand why they might have that concern. But it doesn't mean they aren't feeling it inside. They still need support and sensitivity." So do not take other's surprise at your disclosure as anything other than a difference in perspective. Two people can share different beliefs and support one another. In fact, anyone who shares your negative body image beliefs is not a helpful support person.

Professional Help

In an ideal situation, we feel connected enough with our providers to share our struggles with body image. If you sense that your provider might collude with your body image issues, consider finding another provider.

If we wrestle with body image issues on a daily basis, we need support. If you have not yet sought out psychotherapy, now is the time. Search for a provider trained in working with eating disorders. Even if you do not feel you have an eating disorder, these folks are most savvy in body image. A deep understanding of these issues is necessary to unpack body image without engaging in collusion. Much of the information on searching for a therapist to treat postpartum disorders (located in Chapter 7 on page 117) applies to finding a therapist who specializes in any particular area, including body image.

Likewise, the case for finding a dietitian who works with body image issues. Marci Evans and I chatted on this issue in our interview. "I think that well-trained dietitians can be incredible resources. As dietitians, our initial training is very limited. We are trained in a very medicalized, prescriptive model that features giving answers and telling people what to do. It takes a lot of additional training to work more like a counselor (which may still feature guidance and providing information), but also working with you in a way that is collaborative." Marci also recommends seeking a dietitian trained in eating disorder work, even if you don't think you have one. "In addition to working through practical pieces such as what you're having for dinner, they're also going to be more psychologically minded to integrate what happens in your own mind and how that interfaces with your life. Also, see if you can find someone with additional training in intuitive eating." For more information on intuitive eating, consult Chapter 5 (page 89) or the Resources section on page 229.

One Last Thing

There is no finish line.

At the beginning of treatment, clients often assume they will end therapy when they no longer experience negative body image. I understand that idea, but it simply is not realistic. We live in a body-obsessed, thin, and youth-idealized culture. We are all affected. All of us have negative body image thoughts at some point. There is no fairy-tale ending where the spell lifts and we never have a disparaging thought about our bodies ever again. However, we can change our relationship to our bodies and body image. We can learn to see how our thoughts alter our perception of our bodies. We can educate ourselves to see when we need more care.

Notes

Bacon, Linda. *Health at Every Size: The Surprising Truth about Your Weight.* BenBella Books, 2010.

Coyne, Sarah, and Toni Liechty. "The Effect of Media on Body Image in Pregnant and Postpartum Women." Health Communication, Volume 33, Issues 7, July 3, 2018.

Coyne, Sarah and Toni Liechty. "Media Mommas: Body Image and Media Consumption." Interview by Corinne Crossley, *Momma Bites! podcast,* March 2020.

Evans, Marci. "Postpartum Body Image." Interview by Corinne Crossley, *Momma Bites! podcast,* April 2020.

Guest-Jelley, Anna. "Curvy Yoga with Anna Guest-Jelley." Interview by Corinne Crossley, *Momma Bites! podcast,* March 2020.

Liechty, Toni, and Sarah Coyne, Kevin Collier, and Audrey Sharp. "It's Just Not Very Realistic": Perceptions of Media among Pregnant and Postpartum Women." Health communication, 33, 7. July 3, 2018.

Monte Nido & Affiliates. "Statistics on Dieting and Eating Disorders." Last accessed: December 1, 2019. https://www.montenido.com/pdf/montenido _statistics.pdf

Reuters. "Global Weight Loss Market 2018 Analysis." January 16, 2018 https://www.reuters.com/brandfeatures/venture-capital/article?id=25242

Chapter 10:

Babyproofing Your Relationship
Taking Care of Your Partnership

Here we are for the one millionth time
Laughing in the face of danger
There you are thank God you're mine
I don't know what I'd do if you were a stranger
—Rhett Miller, "You Were a Stranger"

When we bring home our babies, we have a great many questions at the fore-front of our minds. *How often will we need to feed her? How will we know if there's something really wrong with him? How long can a human go without a good night's sleep?* But a question we may not dare ask aloud is *How is this baby about to change my relationship?*

"This time in life is a really unique experience," Patrice Carroll, LICSW, a couples therapist specializing in attachment theory, begins in our *Momma Bites!* podcast interview. "Couples come into this time with joy, hope, and excitement. They just want to do the best for themselves, their partners, and this new little one they brought into the world." Most of us do not factor in the simultaneous adjustment to our partnerships along with the experience of new parenthood. Our partnerships are sailing into uncharted territory.

Patrice's interest in working with couples began with individual work with postpartum moms. "I found a lot of the conversations I had with women focused on the relationships they were in; situations where they felt distressed or stuck. They felt misunderstood, confused, or scared in what they were going through. They needed their partners to understand more about that, so I started inviting these relationships into the room. With this approach, I found we could do a lot more both in the understanding of my clients and their relationships. If one person in the relationship isn't doing well, then the relationship isn't doing well."

Connection versus Deprivation

"Human beings are wired for connection," Patrice explains. "When this connection is in distress, we start to struggle both as individuals and in relationships. When everything is new for a postpartum couple, things can get turned around pretty quickly. However, if a couple fully understands how they can really show up for one another, then we do better in each of the changes of life."

It is easy to see how a relationship can become rapidly distressed in the postpartum era. "With babies needing so much, both partners can fall into states of deprivation. In deprivation, what helps us most is to turn to our partner we count on to reassure or comfort us. But when a couple is in deprivation, the relationship is in deprivation." But I promise you, deterioration does not have to be your default destination. We can start turning this tide today.

Active Listening Skills

Cassie was at her wits' end. She could not remember the last time she had a good night's sleep. A normal part of life with her first baby, this is something she'd expected with her second child. But the symptoms she experienced with the lack of sleep with her five-month-old felt different. Moreover, it affected her ability to exercise. With a moderate anxiety prior to having children, she found exercise to be essential for mental health.

In previous sessions, we discussed some recent behaviors surfacing for Cassie in the last few weeks. Irritability, entitlement, anxiety, muscle pain, and mindless eating all showed as flags of deprivation. As homework, I urged her to talk with her husband about these as signs, and perhaps invite him to consider ways that he was in deprivation as well.

"So, I talked with Austin, as assigned," she announced at the start of session. As typical with anxious clients, Cassie never dared forget to do her homework.

"And . . ."

"At first, it sucked. When we started talking, it felt like a bit of a martyrs' competition. As I started naming ways that I knew I was depleted, he started naming his as well. I know that was sort of the point, but I started to get pissed. I wanted to say, 'Are you kidding me? I nurse this kid all night and *you* feel tired in the morning?' But I kept that for my inside voice," she says as we chuckle. "It was really hard to do that active listening thing, but I tried my best," she reiterates, referring to the skills we had discussed around listening to one's partner, rather than waiting to speak (discussed later in this chapter).

"What happened when you were able to use those skills?"

"Well, I was actually able to hear him. But even before that, since we weren't as defensive with each other, he came to understand what he had not realized before."

"What's that?"

"He hadn't fully understood how important working out has become for me. I just figured he knew. I've always been active but I guess I hadn't been clear with him on how stark the difference is when I exercise versus when I don't. I would've thought he noticed, and he had a bit, but he didn't know that it can be the major difference between me feeling like I'm going to lose it or not."

I want to highlight a few points here that illustrate much of what our couples expert, Patrice Carroll offered. Clearly Cassie, as with many moms, was stuck in deprivation mode for quite a while. In said mode, she pulled further into herself and felt urges to compete with her husband for who felt most deprived. The difference-maker here was her willingness to steer away from deprivation mode and point herself toward connection. Rather than going into an attack mode (consistent with a competitive relationship) she was able to open up about her experience, helping her partner to understand her needs.

Let's talk about the active listening skills Cassie mentioned. What is active listening and why does it matter? Active listening is a basic, but sometimes difficult, practice. These are the foundational techniques therapists learn on day one of our education. If you find a good connection with a therapist who actively listens, you should feel heard, focused on, and validated. Here's how we do it:

- **Look at the person who is speaking.** Make eye contact. Show them that you are engaged.

- **Listen to their words.** Sounds simple? It isn't. Often when people are talking with us, we are thinking about other things (namely, how we're about to respond). Ask questions or for clarification if there are things you wish to understand better.

- **Show them that you heard what they said.** Repeat it back to them. Begin the reflection (the therapeutic term for this) by saying "So, what I heard you say was . . . " or "This is what I'm hearing, can I check it out with you?" This disarms defensiveness. If we feel seen and heard, we are less likely to stay vigilant to our own "side" of the issue.

- **Validate.** When you authentically see the other person's point of view, validate it. This does not mean you agree with it, but rather that you can see it from their perspective. However, if you do not see it from their side, don't pretend. That's patronizing. Even children easily pick up on this type of inauthenticity. Think of when you've felt patronized—it can be enraging and leave us feeling unsafe. We get the message this is not a person who hears us or can be trusted with our vulnerability. If you don't see it from their perspective, it's okay to acknowledge that, while also reminding them this is not a terminal condition. For example, we could say "I'm still struggling to understand XYZ, but I'm trying and I want to."

- **Shampoo, rinse, repeat.** As often as possible in your interactions, practice active listening. This becomes a model for your partner as well. It also creates a lot more space to ask for the same sort of courtesy from them.

Reprioritizing Your Relationship

Now everyone dreams of love lasting and true
Oh, but you and I know what this world can do
So let's make our steps clear that the other may see

I'll wait for you
And if I should fall behind
Wait for me
—Bruce Springsteen, "If I Should Fall Behind"

So why all the coaching about putting your listening ears on? Because we forget. In this tired, baby-obsessed year, we can lose touch with one another. It's not because we don't care for one another—quite the contrary. Often this happens because we love and trust our partner so fully, we de-prioritize our partnerships. This de-prioritization is not intentional—it is survival. In survival mode, we can get entrenched in ineffective communication patterns. "Fundamentally, that's because couples have lost time with one another. It takes time and good intention to slow down, take a moment, really listen, or hug a little longer." Patrice reminds us.

"Just to keep the functionality going, couples sometimes end up sleeping in separate bedrooms. They set up a tag team of 'you go this way and I'll go that way.' Lately, I hear more couples taking turns on family leave time to keep the baby home longer. Moms stay home first while the partner goes to work, then the partner stays home while mom goes back to work. That's a beautiful system for the baby, but it is difficult on the bond with one another. There is no space for each partner's welfare or what they need from their relationship to maintain a steady connection. Even when couples have to tag team, we must find ways to keep checking in with each other and be emotionally available for one another, even just to be vulnerable with one another, to say, 'I miss you.'"

The relationship struggles Patrice describes are so easy to fall into. How can we resist these patterns of relationship neglect? After all, we need to keep the trains running on time, as do our partners. "The result of less connection time is a slow deterioration of the couple's emotional responsiveness for one another. We respond less from a place of emotional connection and go into a fight-or-flight response. Consequently, couples start to disconnect in their relationship, even at times where they feel more successful managing post-partum life."

Date Night, Eye Contact, and Other Methods for Reconnecting

"When's the last time you guys had some time together, just the two of you?" I ask Olive in response to her disclosed frustration in her marriage.

She laughs. "Ummmm ... when we were working on our taxes last month?" she offers, shrugging. "I tried to make it nice. We ordered in and I poured some wine."

"Nice, but I'm not sure that's enough right now. It seems like you need some reconnection time."

"Ugh, I know. We're just so exhausted all the time with the baby. And it's great that the business took off during this time, but it feels even more impossible to connect now. Not to mention everything a night out entails—dressing up, planning, a babysitter."

"Woah, wait. Who said anything about going out? Didn't you just say that your together time was over taxes? I doubt you were doing that out at a restaurant."

"Well, no. You mean, we could do that at home?"

"Why not? You ordered in for taxes? Why not do the same thing just for a chance to connect?"

I often advocate for at-home date nights for my clients and their partners with small children. Financial constraints, unreadiness to leave the baby, and lack of a sitter all prevent nights out. At-home date nights can be a more purposeful way to set aside time for the relationship. It does not have to be weekly or anything fancy. Just some time that you set aside to be with your partner.

Steps for date night:

- **Set parameters.** Set a time and date, e.g., this Friday after the kids are in bed. Make some plans for the 'date.' Dinner? Netflix? Board game?

- **Show up.** Do about a third of what would make you feel good to go out with your spouse. Pull on a sweater over your nursing bra. Brush your teeth. Put on shoes. Or don't. Whatever works for you.
- **Set boundaries.** No kid-talk? No phones?
- **Be realistic.** This won't be perfect. No date is perfect. You may struggle with distraction. You may have to nurse in the middle. Your two-year-old could throw up in the middle of it. It doesn't have to lead to sex. You will fall asleep during the movie. It's not about falling in love all over again—it's about intentional time together.

Date Night Ideas

- Cooking together.
- Short movie and then chat about the movie.
- Glass of wine (or some enjoyable beverage) on the couch while you chat (about things other than breastmilk and paternity leave).
- Trying a new (or old favorite) board game.
- Order in. Put it on plates. Light candles.

If you want to set fire to this book at the idea of adding another thing to your already overfull plate, I get it. Date nights do not have to be your way back to one another, I promise. Whatever you do does not matter. However you create more space for your relationship is fine. Patrice offers, "It's about creating time. Try not to get overwhelmed and think 'that means a weekend away or going out.' It's more about holding onto one another just a little bit longer before you say goodbye in the morning. When your partner comes into the room, connect with them in a way that shows them you notice them. Create intention to demonstrate the message *You are so important to me, I don't know how I would do this without you.*"

Acting Out: Couples Behaving Badly

Brooke: "I want you to want to do the dishes."

Gary: "Why would I want to do dishes?"

—Jennifer Aniston and Vince Vaughn in *The Break-Up*

"Ugh! He doesn't get it! He thinks I'm crazy with this cereal thing, but I'm not," Lena says, reiterating the argument she had with her husband over the difference between rice and oatmeal cereal. "I don't want to give her rice cereal. I'm worried she's going to get all backed-up again like she was last month."

"You were frustrated that he brought home rice instead of oatmeal," I reflect.

"Yes! I mean, in some ways I get how it happened. The brand we use only has a difference in font color for the rice versus the oatmeal. I realize how he grabbed the wrong one. I never thought it was intentional. I just got upset because he didn't get why I didn't want to feed her the stuff he got."

"He didn't understand the difference."

"No. But you know what? He doesn't have to understand the difference. I just needed him to back me up. It was the fact that he had to debate me about it, when I just needed him to support me."

"What could he have done to support you? Did you want him to go back out?"

"No, I felt bad asking him to do that. As it was, it was my fault for forgetting the oatmeal on the grocery shop. But then he didn't want me to go back out to get the oatmeal. He said that I have enough to do without running back to the store for such a small difference."

"So, he might have been trying to be supportive?"

"But that's not how I needed him to support me. It would have been more helpful for him to say 'that sucks, babe' when I went back out to the store, but instead he kept telling me not to go. I know it's childish, but I got super annoyed, so I just pulled away. We didn't talk the rest of the night. Over oatmeal," she says rolling her eyes.

"This reminds me of when you were thinking about your job change a few months ago, and you wanted him to be in your corner, rather than helping you parse out all the potential pros and cons."

"Exactly! See? This comes up all the time."

"So, it seems like silent treatment over cereal, but it's really a disconnect between what you want and what he's offering."

"How do you mean?"

"Well, you want him in your corner unquestioningly. Whereas, for him, he may see challenging the way you think about things as being supportive."

Lena considers this at length. "He does do that, doesn't he? Sometimes it's helpful but in times like this, it drives me crazy. It feels like he's debating me just to make me nuts."

Lena and her husband are not alone in their relationship struggles. Patrice explains, "Couples can start to loop around in the same argument. It might have a different story to it like 'I told you to take out the trash' or 'I told you I was going out tonight, you were supposed to be with the baby' but when they keep falling into the same argument, usually something deeper is going on. In distress, we bring our tendencies in to protect ourselves."

What are these tendencies? Patrice outlines two interdependent roles: the pursuer and the withdrawer. The member of the couple who assumes the pursuit role is desperate to maintain connection. "This can even look like fighting or blaming. Their underlying message is *I would rather fight with you than have no connection at all. No connection frightens me the most.*" Pursuers can appear like they want to keep a conflict going, even coming off as they 'want the last word' but it is the connection they are trying to keep alive.

If we have a pursuer, we must also have a withdrawer. "Withdrawal tendency is characterized by conflict avoidance. This partner wishes to preserve the connection. They are so afraid of making it worse, they assume the conflict is their fault. When they sense distress, withdrawers dial down interaction. Their withdrawal appears distant or apathetic. They might say things like 'it's fine,' or 'it will get better' but this is coming from a flight tendency.

They are trying to neutralize the playing field, hoping the distress will pass and a better day will come," Patrice explains. "This turns the couple into what we call a negative interactional cycle," Patrice validates. "They get stuck in it. It doesn't matter what the content is—it could be anything and everything, but the cycle is the same."

Getting Help

"What would you think of couples therapy?" I ask Lena, who instantly looks alarmed with my question.

"You think things are that bad? It was just a little argument over oatmeal," she says, half-laughing.

"It's not that I think things are so concerning between the two of you. But you named it yourself. You just want him to be in your corner, unconditionally. When you feel that he isn't, it feels awful and you withdraw. He gets angry. You feel pissed at him for being angry, so you pull away more. This seems like a repetitive pattern of communication that is hurting you both."

"It does seem that way. But is therapy really necessary?"

People often feel freaked-out when I bring up couples therapy. There are a couple of reasons I refer people for this type of treatment. One is for support dealing with a crisis or trauma. Couples therapy can be tremendously helpful in these situations. Each individual manages with events in their own way. A therapist can serve as a conduit for effective communication within the couple.

I also refer couples for support even when they are not dealing with a major crisis. In these situations, couples are stuck in unhelpful communication patterns. Otherwise, they function well. No one is having an affair. No one is threatening divorce. When I recommend couples work, I simply offer the idea that more support from an unbiased party can be a helpful thing. In contrast with individual work, the relationship is the client in couples therapy. In any therapeutic treatment with more than one person (couples therapy, family therapy) it is the relationship (or relationships in the case of a family) that is the client, rather than any particular person. "When couples are moving around in their times of distance, disconnection, or conflict, they need help. Why wouldn't they? That's normal. It's okay to get stuck. It is not okay to stay stuck. That stuckness gets rigid, creating rifts where we associate one another with automatic responses like 'I know you're not going to agree with me anyway,' or 'You don't believe what I'm saying to you.' Usually those statements are loaded with a lot of hurt and sadness, but what comes out instead is blame and shame. If this cycle goes on too long, it erodes a sense of safety in a couple. That being said, even in that situation, I have worked with couples in negative cycles for years. They may be surprised at the length of time they work with me, but slowly they start to find their way back to one another. It happens in a beautiful way that I get to witness over and over again," Patrice explains.

Some good leads on couples therapy:
- As with other providers, ask your OB or midwife for resources.
- Look for a postpartum specialist. If they don't specialize in couples work, ask them for a referral.
- Ask friends, family, and people you feel safe with for their recommendations.

Notes

Carroll, Patrice. "Your Postpartum Partnership with Patrice Carroll, LICSW." Interview by Corinne Crossley *Momma Bites! podcast,* October 25, 2019.

Miller, Rhett. "You Were a Stranger." On The Messenger. New York City, NY: ATO Records, 2018. CD.

Springsteen, Bruce. "If I Should Fall Behind." On Lucky Town. Columbia Records, 1992. CD.

Vaughn, Vincent. (producer), & Reed, P. (director). (2006). *The Break-up* United States: Mosaic Media Group. Motion Picture.

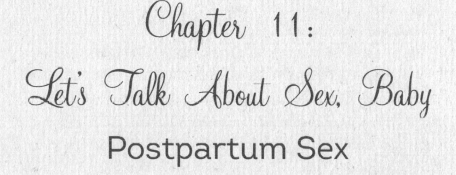

Chapter 11:

Let's Talk About Sex, Baby

Postpartum Sex

"Well, you look great!" my midwife says, pulling off her gloves, as I sit up and gather the giant, novelty sized paper napkin drape at my waist. I am at my six-week postpartum check-up appointment, which I've passed with flying colors. "You can start having sex again," she tells me.

"Oh. Good." I reply, trying to manage a smile. Sex. Six weeks postpartum, back to work, nursing, and pumping—sex is about as appealing as dragging my nails across a chalkboard.

"Take it slow. Make sure you use plenty of lube. Remember, you're nursing. That dries you out."

"Well, that's good to know!" I say, happy for concrete advice.

I leave the office and drive home, scanning my body for even the faintest of erotic stirrings. Nothing. I feel fiercely protective of my breasts and milk supply and can barely stand when anyone hugs me, never mind if I were to be sexual. I recoil a bit at the thought.

I wish I'd known then how common this experience is for new mothers.

"I was relatively youngish for having kids," Sarah Swofford, author of *From Ouch! to Ahhh . . . The New Mom's Guide to Sex After Baby*, tells me in our *Momma Bites!* podcast interview. "I was twenty-six years old, a sex educator, and after my son was born, I was blown away by how my desire disappeared. I thought something was inherently broken in me. I went to look for books to figure out what to do. I went to libraries, bookstores—there was nothing. The only thing I found were Cosmo-like articles about how to make yourself look good for your man. Then when I went to a male ob/gyn and told him 'I just don't want to ever have sex and I always used to. I know I had the baby months ago, but it still hurts.' His response was 'Well, you know, if you don't use it, you lose it.' I knew that could not be the answer."

This is far from uncommon. In 2000, a research survey of 484 new moms revealed that 83 percent reported pain with sex (known as dyspareunia) within the first three months of their postpartum year. That number dropped to 64 percent at the six-month mark, but remained well over pre-pregnancy norms. "Most couples have sexual difficulties and challenges after giving birth. Sexual challenges are the norm after having a baby. The concept of this being something bad needs to change to something normal," Sarah validates.

"As women we are so socialized to believe that if we can't fix something, it is our fault. We rarely feel good enough. There's always something that needs to be better or fixed. Especially in sexuality, which often incorporates another person where we feel responsible for another's sexual needs."

You are not broken. Postpartum bodies often need time and practice, but we struggle to offer this to ourselves. Assuming all the responsibility for your relationship's sexual satisfaction is counterproductive. Prioritizing your partner's satisfaction over your own is a major mistake. So, what can we do?

Honor the Situation

It can be hard not to panic when sex is both a method of connection with our partners and an expected behavior in our role as women. Prior to having a baby, the experience of sex might be where we felt most embodied, only to find ourselves entirely disconnected from this feeling postpartum. How could we not freak out?

Let's talk about some things that can extinguish desire.

Hormone Changes

Ahhh, pregnancy and postpartum—not since middle school have we been on such a hormonal roller coaster. As we give birth, and (in some cases) start nursing, estrogen and progesterone levels drop. This is necessary and beneficial for our babies, but can wreak a bit of havoc on our sexual desire. Progesterone's drop tells our bodies to make milk for our babies. At the same time, decreases in estrogen leave us dried out. "Estrogen is found in every tissue of the body and is responsible for lubrication," according to Kimberly Ann Johnson in her book *The Fourth Trimester: A Postpartum Guide to Healing Your Body, Balancing Your Emotions & Restoring Your Vitality* (Johnson 2017, 114). Hence my midwife's advice. In addition to lack of lubrication, hormones can also be the culprit behind painful sex. If you experience pain with sex, consult your doctor. Much like other postpartum issues (especially mood disorders) do not try to suffer through it hoping it will get better. Your body, your partner, and your sex life all deserve better than that.

Stress

"Your body is undergoing a stress response for many months, if not a year," Sarah says, affirming what we already know in our bodies. "All the research shows that the minute you have stress, the first thing to disappear is sexual desire." Is there a more distracting time than your postpartum year? We are obsessed with sleep and feeding, and are in an activated mode of protection. None of these make space for sex. Sex is the ultimate mindfulness activity. Being distracted or pulled in other directions is an immediate desire-killer.

My absolute favorite work around understanding female sexuality is that of Emily Nagoski, PhD, sex educator and author of *Come As You Are: The Surprising New Science That Will Transform Your Sex Life*. It is my firm belief that this book should be required reading for anyone with a vagina and anyone who wants to have sex with one. In addition to explaining desire (which we will discuss shortly), she also explains the role of stress in our sex lives. If we want to feel turned on, Nagoski explains that we need to both take our foot off the sexual brakes (stress) and put it on the sexual accelerator (positive context).

Postpartum mom's short list of possible sources of stress (which inhibit sexual desire):
- Lack of sleep
- Worry about the baby
- Worry the baby will wake up or need something while mom is having sex
- Body image issues
- Feeling behind or unable to keep up with life demands
- Lack of self-care/time for oneself

Did I say worry? In her book, Nagoski explains: "Stressed out humans more readily interpret all stimuli as threats. We also know that the brain can handle only a limited amount of information at a time; at its simplest, we can think of stress as information overload" (Nagoski 2015, 117-118). Postpartum moms are already so filled with stress of baby care and emotional labor, sexual overtures are often more overstimulating than welcome.

So, what's a mom to do? It is not like stress is about to go out of our lives in the foreseeable future. Again, we arrive at the necessity of self-care. While it seems easier to push stress away to get in the mood, it doesn't work. Nagoski's metaphor of taking our foot off our sexual brakes is apt. The more pressure we put on ourselves to get in the mood, the more we stomp on the brakes. If our foot is already fully on the brakes, expecting ourselves to override this feeling to get turned on is essentially flooring the accelerator with the brakes fully engaged. What happens? We rev our engines and go nowhere. Instead, we need to find ways to discharge some of the stress in our lives by taking our foot off the brakes.

Nagoski advises the importance of allowing our bodies to discharge our stress cycles with movement. I wholeheartedly agree with this intervention for a number of reasons. First, movement helps discharge stress chemicals in our bodies and promote helpful neurochemicals like endorphins. Second, movement helps us connect back into our bodies. Much of the stress named above is emotional and psychological in nature. The resolution is to get out of our heads, yet staying stuck in our minds just keeps the stress engine running. Grounding into our bodies opens us to the opportunity to notice and experience pleasure.

Letting go of stress is not like throwing off a wet blanket. It can recede slowly at times. Do not feel discouraged if your efforts to move through your stress response do not initially feel life-changing. Learning how to manage stress is a lifelong skill for moms. Keep listening to your body and honoring it. This is the path to an enjoyable sex life.

Getting Turned On

A groundbreaking aspect of Nagoski's book is its normalization of female desire. For women, lack of desire is simultaneously widely accepted and pathologized. That's an unusual pairing. Usually pathologized traits are considered abnormal. But when it comes to the idea of a woman with a low libido, the jokes are as old as cave drawings. Nagoski's book takes apart misconceptions by examining how human beings experience desire. She outlines two types of desire—spontaneous desire and responsive desire. Most of us think spontaneous desire is the only type of desire—how our bodies are "supposed to" work. Just as it sounds, spontaneous desire hits us suddenly out of nowhere, and we are turned on. According to Nagoski, spontaneous desire occurs in "75 percent of men and 15 percent of women" (Nagoski 2015, 225).

"The spontaneous desire style is so privileged in our culture, so valued, that it's easy to feel disempowered if that's not your primary style," Nagoski writes (Nagoski 2015, 229). This is one of the major reasons that we misunderstand and pathologize responsive desire. Responsive desire describes those of us who experience the wish for sex "only after sexy things are already happening," according to Nagoski (225). In this particular situation, she explains that "desire comes along when arousal meets a great context." Translation: We get turned on when we have a stimulating situation that activates both our bodies and minds (arousal), and are in a favorable situation and state of mind (context). For the 30 percent of women and 5 percent of men with responsive desire, context (our state of mind and situation) are especially important. These are also the sources with the highest potential activation of our sexual brakes. So, if we experience responsive desire, we must make sure our sexual brakes (stress, anxiety, fatigue) are off, and our sexual accelerator (safety, connection, relaxation) is on. The more things in the way of creating a favorable state of mind, the less likely we are to respond. Nagoski reminds us: "Responsive desire is normal and healthy ... it turns out everyone's sexual desire is responsive and context dependent. It just *feels* more spontaneous for some and more responsive for others" (Nagoski 2015, 225).

Reconnecting with Your Sexual Self

As you can see, the road to feeling turned on is more a matter of correctly lining up dominoes rather than a magical spell where we are spirited away. Knowing how to set up our dominoes comes from understanding our turn-ons and turn-offs. Just as it is important to know what sources of stress squash our libido, it is important to get in touch with the things that we like.

As you begin to explore (or further explore) what you like most sexually, be gentle with yourself. Sex is not necessarily a source of pleasure for every person. Returning to sex when we have a history of trauma must be done so respectfully and compassionately. This includes birth trauma. We can forget that a traumatic birth can affect our sex lives, but of course it can. If you find returning to sexual activity or exploring sources of pleasure to be triggering, please reach out for therapeutic support as soon as possible. Refer to Chapter 7 (page 117) and Chapter 10 (page 181) for tips on finding the right fit for individual or couples therapy.

Do you feel aware of what you like? Is your partner aware of what you like and do not like? In *From Ouch! to Ahhh . . . The New Mom's Guide to Sex After Baby*, Sarah Swofford advocates exploring our likes and dislikes as a way of stocking our "arousal toolbox." "Sex can be so glorious and fun. That's why we like doing it and beat ourselves up when we're not doing it. Part of the idea of sexual ownership is to become an expert in yourself and your vitality. Explore what lights you up, and then apply that to getting your libido excited. What turns you on is yours. And it changes. Building the arousal toolbox takes self-care and work. It is about caressing ourselves, loving ourselves, finding time to masturbate. It's taking the time to look at our partner and find the things that are delicious about them, and then telling them directly 'I would love it if you did this,' or 'I would like to do this.' That's how we build our arousal toolbox."

Self-Love

"It's tempting to think *if my partner really loves me, they will do this thing* or *if they care enough, they'll know what my needs are and fulfill me sexually.* Instead, we need to take some radical responsibility for ourselves. We cannot control how someone else behaves. People can disappoint us. Our partners can disappoint us. They can make us feel like they don't care. This leads to resentment. Resentment is a killer of love and desire. Our responsibility is in identifying what we need and like. That doesn't mean something that someone else is going to give to us—it is figuring out how we are going to give that to ourselves," Sarah offers.

One way to build our sexual toolbox is through touch. The gold standard work for reconnecting couples dealing with sexual issues is through non-demand touch. This type of touch is just as it sounds. Consider using the same exercise for exploring touch with yourself. Pursuing this type of touch is to explore your sexual likes and dislikes. In contrast to non-demand touch exercises for couples, the hope is that we learn to touch ourselves in ways that feel erotic. If this is too uncomfortable for you, start with the most basic forms of touch. What sensations are most pleasurable to you? What fabrics feel best on your skin? What touches make you feel most comforted?

If you are comfortable with the idea of sexual touch, consider what sensations feel most pleasurable to you. What type of clothes make you feel (not look) sexy? When you masturbate or touch yourself in a sexual way, what areas of your body feel most receptive and cause the most excitement? This is an especially important exploration in the postpartum era, as you may experience touch entirely differently since having a baby. Caring for a baby, fatigue, and nursing are just a few of the many elements that affect our experience of touch. Knowing how motherhood has changed our experience of touch (at least for now) is a helpful source of information before we even consider involving a partner. "What does desire feel like if you don't even consider another person? What if it's just about you and what you like, want, and need—you desiring yourself?" Sarah asks.

A Word on Body Image

A major source of sexual brakes for many women in the postpartum year is their relationship with their body image. With our bodies feeling like strangers, it is very difficult to feel embodied and powerful (a major aphrodisiac). The temptation to put off sex (and lots of other things) until we are in the "right" kind of body is ill-advised. "The idea that the smaller you are, the more worthy you are of love, does not serve us. If we are feeling alien in our bodies, we must give ourselves permission to consider 'what makes me feel good?' rather than focusing on how our bodies look," Sarah offers. As stated earlier, the more we focus on how our bodies look, the more out of step we get with what feels good.

Reconnecting with Your Partner

"The people who reach out and contact me the most about my book are cisgender men. They don't understand what is happening—why their sexual relationship has changed so much and they want to understand. So much of a sexual relationship is learning how to have healthy sexual communication and honoring our sexual selves."

—Sarah Swofford

As we saw from the beginning of this chapter, sexual issues are incredibly common in the postpartum year. If fact, they are the norm. Just as we need skills in our arousal toolbox as individuals, we also need a set of strategies for sexual interactions with our partners. These skills are written to address committed partner relationships, but many are still transferable to polyamorous or other types of relationships. However, for ease of reading (and writing), this chapter will predominantly focus on committed relationships.

Sex(y) Talk

"You should know something," I tell my husband while pouring myself some cereal.

"What's that?" he asks, taking the milk out of the refrigerator.

"You know how when I'm nursing, I don't really love being touched?"

"I do."

"It's not just you. I don't love being hugged or anything like that."

"I remember."

"I really appreciate how respectful you've been about that."

"I try."

"I can tell." I pause while I slice strawberries and try to gather my words. "It might seem like overkill, but I feel like I need to let you know the extent of the situation."

"Okay . . ."

"I think you should know that anytime you even accidentally brush one of my boobs, I have this instantaneous urge to break your nose."

"My nose?"

"Jason Stathum-style."

"Jason Stathum?"

"You know when he's like kicking ass or defending the life of some helpless person? You know how he does that move . . . "

" . . . like with the heel of his hand? And blood comes pouring out of the guy's face?" he asks, his eyes wide.

"Exactly."

"But I don't even go near your . . . "

"I know," I say, cutting him off. "It's only for a millisecond, but even with an incidental touch. It's there. That feeling like I want to break your nose. Stathum-style. I just wanted you to know."

"Great."

Our experience of sex changes after having a baby. Touch feels different. Roles feel different. The relationship feels different. The best way we can evolve with this is to talk about it with our partners. As you can see from my interaction with my husband, sexual communication is not always easy and comfortable. Sometimes it is awkward. Sometimes it is arousing. Sometimes it feels purely logistical. It is still important. Even this interaction, which may sound silly to you, ended up being helpful (as well as a running joke). Until the moment I shared this experience with him, I felt alone in my instant rage (clearly a physiological reaction to nursing). When I shared it with him, I felt less alone. I also felt he could hold an equal amount of caution as I did in physical interactions.

"The postpartum year is this one crazy, psychedelic year," Sarah Swofford offers. "Nothing else is going to be the way it is in this one, intense moment of life. But the rest of your life will have these times when things are constantly changing. That is part of long-term partnerships. We learn to surf those waves by building a good base of communication, setting boundaries, and feeling respected." A logistical way communication is important is managing sexual boundaries. Especially in the postpartum year (but actually at all points throughout our lives) we need to be clear with our partners on what we want and do not want, as well as how we do and do not want to be touched in physical (even non-sexual) interactions. This is an excellent opportunity for both of you to discuss what feels best in physical touch.

Another motive for sexual communication is protective against obligatory sex dynamics. "Something I hear over and over again is the idea of sex as duty," Sarah says. There are few dynamics less sexy than obligation to service one's partner. In the realm of couples, the opposite of obligation is curiosity. Obligation equates to expectation. In the state of curiosity, few things are assumed. As with so many skills in this book, curiosity is a superpower level skill in a couple's arousal toolbox. Too often we get stuck in our sexual patterns. From well-established roles, to old-standby sex positions, it is easy to get the record needle stuck in the same groove. Yet, a little curiosity and openness go a long way, as Sarah explains. "Sex doesn't have to be with the purpose of having intercourse. It doesn't have to be a penis in a vagina. Arousal, desire, and sex are so much more than that. When we focus on that, we're selling everyone short. We need to look at it as sharing arousal and sexuality. I think a lot of new parents would have a lot more sexual connection if they would expand their sexual definition. They would realize that there are so many more moments of sexual connection when you take away the pressure of sexual intercourse. Once you know your arousal toolbox, finding the ways to share the pieces you want to share is important. Our partners need to be taught, just like we need to be taught about them. It's a privilege and an honor. "

Remember that gold standard treatment to a couple's sexual issues? Non-demand touching is a great example of curiosity in action. The idea with non-demand touch for couples is to take the pressure of sex off the table. Couples can benefit from taking time to reconnect physically, intimately, without the assumption of sex. Think of it like an athlete cross-training. NFL quarterbacks do not hone their skills only by throwing footballs. They run, lift, do functional training, and practice yoga. Our intercourse game will only benefit from a bit of sexual cross-training with curiosity.

Compassion is Sexy

It is hard enough to find time to share a pizza in the postpartum year, let alone have sex. Allow yourselves time. This is a significant evolution in your relationship. Be gentle with yourselves and each other. Forcing sex is only going to make it suck in the long-term.

No matter how perfectly matched, everyone has disappointing sex sometimes. Have compassion for yourself and your partner. Sarah advises, "Try to have a sense of humor about it. You can say, 'well we've done better than that!' but also remember that this will pass. You're in this really hard time and it will get better. There are times when sex is just about sharing your love, connection, gentleness, and physical affection. Honor those needs, rather than just the idea that you need to get back on the horse. That's not good for anybody." Honor your bodies. Be nice.

Notes

Barrett, G., *Women's Sexual Health after Childbirth*, https://www.ncbi.nlm .nih.gov/pubmed/10688502 BJOG, 2000, February; (107) 2

Johnson, Kimberly Ann. *The Fourth Trimester: A Postpartum Guide to Healing Your Body, Balancing Your Emotions, and Restoring Your Vitality.* Boulder: Shambhala, 2017.

Nagoski, Emily. *Come As You Are: The Surprising New Science That Will Transform Your Sex Life*. New York: Simon & Schuster Paperbacks, 2015.

Swofford, Sarah. *From Ouch! to Ahhh . . . The New Mom's Guide to Sex After Baby*. Sarah J Swofford Media, 2014.

Swofford, Sarah. "Postpartum Sex Chat with Sarah Swofford." Interview by Corinne Crossley, *Momma Bites! podcast*, August 8, 2019.

Chapter 12:

. . . and Everybody Else

Friendships, Family Connections & Other Relationships

"I've got to say something to my dad," May admits in session.

"Oh no, what now?" I ask, bracing for another devastating fat-phobic comment, as I am accustomed to hearing in stories about May's interactions with her father.

"It's Talia. She's still so little and he's already got shit to say about her body. We were FaceTiming the other day and I was telling my parents how she's trying to crawl, but having some trouble getting going. So he says, "It's probably because she's so chunky, it's hard to get all that chub moving." I wince and May grows tearful. "Maybe if someone else said something like that, I might even think it's funny. I mean she is a solid little turkey, but all I can hear is the way he talked to me and my sisters about our weight. Don't even get me started on his comments to my mom."

May has struggled with her weight for much of her life. When she began therapy with me, she was restricting and purging on a daily basis. She worked tirelessly on her recovery, even before becoming pregnant. Some of the steps in her recovery process found her moving away from her very close relationship with her dad, allowing herself to take space from their usual Sunday morning coffee routine, during which he made negative comments about her body. Yet, despite creating some helpful distance in the relationship, May found herself unable to put boundaries into words. After entire sessions of role-playing and practicing limit-setting, she would return to session in the subsequent weeks, having been unable to speak those words to him. Now something has shifted.

"What do you want to say to him?"

"Shut the fuck up! She is a baby!"

"That's a good start. Is that how you want to say it to him?"

"No. I know that I'd lose my nerve if I planned to do that. But I feel like if I don't say something soon, I'm going to explode and it's going to be something like that. Which . . . whatever. But I know if I scream at him, I'm going to be the one apologizing and feeling guilty. Then we're right back here where we started."

"So, what could you say to him that feels manageable?"

She thinks for a long time. Several ticks of my office clock pass before she answers.

"I don't know how I can get the nerve to say this, but something like 'Dad, I need you to not talk about Talia's weight. Not around her. Not to me.'"

"That sounds like a reasonable request."

"But I have no idea how I can get the nerve to say it."

"Do you have to *say* it?"

"What do you mean? You've been after me forever to set limits with him."

"I know, but there are all sorts of ways to set limits. Do you think it would be easier in person? How about starting the conversation via email or on the phone? This doesn't have to be a single conversation if you feel that's too overwhelming."

"Starting it off with an email does sound a tiny bit easier."

Boundaries and Families

Even in the closest and most loving of families, we need to set boundaries. The arrival of a baby can be an instant change to your values. Having kids brings these into sharp focus, sometimes causing long-standing conflicts to come to a head quickly. In May's case, she was no longer willing to expose herself or her baby to her father's body-shaming narratives. After a lifetime of trying to justify his criticisms of her sisters, mother, and herself, she was finally able to see how inappropriate his comments were once he was talking about her daughter. In other cases, it might not feel so clear.

Boundaries are essential to relationships. Without boundaries, we become burned-out with one another. Without boundaries, we become exhausted at managing both our own feelings and other's emotions. Boundaries actually help support longer-term relationships. Yet, setting limits can be intimidating. We worry that what we have to say could cause others pain or fall on deaf ears.

Survival strategies for setting limits:

- **Establishing boundaries early makes it easier to circle back to them.** Setting limits in the heat of the moment is fraught. When tempers are high, it can be difficult to parse out words said in anger versus those meant to be meaningful over time. Returning to a previously set limit is infinitely easier than starting from scratch.

- **Do not feel that you have to set all the limits at once.** If you feel empowered to do so, go for it. But if you feel ill at the very thought of setting even a single limit with someone you love, remember, you can simply start with a conversation or statement.

- **Reinforce.** When something unexpected happens, most of us need to hear it again a couple of times before it sinks in. That is a human learning process. While possibly irritating, expect to have to reinforce your message.

- **Plan for testing.** I remember when I was a kid and we were in the grocery store, if I asked my mom for something three times, she would usually give in. While I did not like how this dance felt (she was clearly annoyed) I still knew just how far to push her for what I wanted. We learn where limits actually are by testing them.

- **Be prepared to follow through with consequences.** Boundaries look all different ways. Ideally, you will be heard and respected by others, but if you are not, remind the person of the consequences. "Janet, I love talking with you about childhood trips to the beach, but if you keep bringing up what's upsetting you about my mom, then I'm going to have to take a break and walk away. That's between you and her." This may be the best we can do in relationships. Accepting people for who they are, the way we are, and our differences in values is healthy.

While May decided to open up the conversation around boundaries with her father via email, an issue arose via FaceTime that she no longer wanted to ignore. Having already spent a few sessions discussing what she wanted to address and some basic scripting of how she wanted to say it, her words were at the ready, even if she had not yet emailed him. But when her father made another comment about her daughter's weight on a FaceTime call, she felt she could wait no longer.

"I told him, "Dad, I really don't like it when you talk about Talia's weight.""

"What did he say?"

"He laughed it off at first and said, 'What's the big deal? She's a baby and has no idea.'"

"Just as you were concerned about."

"Yeah, but it really wasn't as bad as how I had been predicting in my head. So, I ended up telling him, "We want you to get used to not saying these kinds of things around Talia, because that's not how we're raising her. We really want her not to hate her body the way most of the people in our family do, so we're not talking that way around her and we need to have the other close people around her not talk about their bodies or any bodies that way.'"

"Woah. Badass!"

"Of course he started to try and argue that the people in our family don't hate their bodies," at which we guffaw, since body hatred in her family is profound. "I told him that it was fine if he didn't see it that way, but as long as he's around Talia, I need him not to talk about people's weight and bodies. He didn't have to agree with it, he just needed to do that one small thing."

"Good for you! How'd it feel?"

"Hard, but not as hard as I thought."

These conversations did not end with this one interaction between May and her dad. He pushed limits and expressed shock when he overstepped a boundary and she held him accountable. It took work, but May reported that slowly things improved. Her father began curtailing some of his negative body talk and even apologized without prompting for some oversteps. Over time, she felt less tense around him. They found things to discuss other than people's appearances and even started meeting for coffee occasionally.

Limits of Help

Just as we must establish boundaries with some connections, we must also respect boundaries. No one person in your village is meant to be able to hold everything—even you. Childcare, emotional support, whatever type of help you need, try to keep your support portfolio diversified. This helps both parties in the relationship. It can keep guilt about putting too much on one person at bay, and it can keep others from feeling exhausted and burnt out with our requests.

When I was pregnant with my daughter, earlier than I expected people began asking us how we were going to manage childcare. We figured that we would enroll her in a couple of days of daycare, my husband could have her while he worked from home for a couple of days (in itself misinformed) and then we assumed my retired in-laws would cover a day. Yet, as my pregnancy progressed, it became clear that this was not their plan. They had vibrant interests and sources of self-care they worked nearly their entire lives to cultivate. Exercising, writing, painting, tutoring, and gardening were all activities central to their days that a baby would render impossible.

In the end, I was glad they did not step into this role. I appreciate their example of their own continued self-care and honoring their own wishes. They provide tremendous support and love to us in other ways while their own needs are met. Their love for their grandchildren is pure and deep. Going to their house still elates my kids. This and many decisions they have made in their lives continue to be a leading example for me of self-care and balance (#lifegoals). While their support did not look as we expected, we feel it profoundly.

Friendships

"I thought I was doing fine," Dr. Sheryl Ziegler, PhD and author of *Mommy Burnout: How to Reclaim Your Life and Raise Healthier Children in the Process*, tells me in our interview. "Every weekend we had plenty of dinner plans, plenty of plans with other families, and lots of events, feeling busy and social all the time. Then one night, I wound up in the hospital, sitting in the ER by myself (my husband was home with the kids because we don't have any family that live in the state to watch them). I noticed that many other people there had someone with them. I was by myself thinking about who I could call to say 'You're never going to believe this, I'm at the hospital, in all this pain, and they're doing tests on me.' I'm not talking about someone that I could say, 'Hey, could you take my kids to school?' I had plenty of those people. But I realized I wasn't grounding myself in my home area. I considered home as where I was from, and those were my people. I didn't have anyone in my state that would care to know what was going on that night. That was a really big shift for me. I really appreciate the value of friendships now. At that time, I had the mentality that everybody I met had to be my instant BFF in order for me to invest in her. Now I respect the power of all different kinds of friendships and do not underestimate the dysfunctional power of loneliness."

In her brilliant book and TED talk, Dr. Ziegler discusses the epidemic of what she coined as "mommy burnout." A central factor fueling burnout in mothers is our isolation. "We are over-tending to our kids and under-befriending our friends." Sheryl illustrated her point with a study that particularly captured her interest around gender differences and stress. "A focus of this study was how different genders manage stress. When we define human fear responses as fight, flight, or freeze; those are actually more male responses. Rather, if we follow our natural tendencies as women, we would actually be tending and befriending. Meaning, when under stress, a woman's natural hormonal tendencies are to tend to her children and befriend other women."

We will discuss a variety of different types of friendships and relationships in this chapter. Intrinsic to each type of connection are benefits and challenges. I invite you to consider your own needs and how to address them with a diversity of connections. Perhaps you are fully stocked on long-term besties known since your pigtail days, but few people you can push your stroller with on Wednesdays. Or perhaps you are trying to manage the ways in which your oldest and dearest relationships are changing with the arrival of your baby.

Consider Dr. Ziegler's own realization after the night she found herself alone in the emergency room. She spoke about how this event changed her perspective around how she saw friendships. She invites moms to consider how "people can serve different needs. In my mind I have many different categories of friend groups. I have my mom-friends, my best friends, I have my go-to friends, and what I call my senior mommies (meaning, they've got kids older than me, they definitely know more than me, and I'm going to go to them for advice). That's a really big shift because I reserved that only for very close friends in the past. Even junior moms, who are younger moms. Because I am an older mom to my third kid, there's lots of them for me. I just listen to them, give them encouragement, and let them know 'I was there, too.' Understanding that I can form really nice friendships with women with kids who are younger and older, that was really big for me."

Child-Free Friends, Mom-Mentors, Milestone Mommies, and Everything in Between

Molly knew her friend Candace would have a hard time once the baby arrived. Candace wore her decision to remain childless as a badge—an important source of her identity. Candace partied hard, drinking into the early hours of morning, about the same time Molly was stumbling toward the bassinet for a midnight feeding. Candace often groused about Molly's decision to "be boring" by having a child, and rolling her eyes at sonogram printouts. Now, Molly expressed concern in therapy about her sense that they were growing apart.

"I've known her forever, but we've always been such different people. I think starting a family is bringing things to a head," Molly says, peering in on her sleeping baby in the car seat she carries into my office every week.

"What do you want from this relationship?" I ask.

"I'm not sure. I still love her. We've always been there for each other. I just don't think we have that much in common. I don't want her to feel that the baby is to blame for our relationship changing."

"What's your concern about that?"

"I just worry that she will resent the baby, even though this has been a long time coming."

"Life circumstances always change our relationships. Parental, sibling, marital, platonic—all of the relationships in our lives evolve all the time. As we age, gain differing experiences, things change in little ways. Having a baby is just something that changes things quickly. The truth is, you've been talking about how this relationship has been changing for years. You know the ways in which things have changed for you. But these might differ in how each of you experience this relationship. You're very different people. You will each define the changes in the relationship in different ways. For you, getting married, buying a house, having a job that you dedicated yourself to and had to be up early in the morning for made you realize that you no longer enjoyed being out drinking all night."

"And once I stopped drinking so much around her, I realized how different we were. I wasn't sure I wanted to keep her so close any more."

"But she may not experience things that way. She might feel that it's the baby's presence that changed the relationship. That's her perspective."

Molly tears up. "I feel bad. She's not a bad person, we just don't have a lot in common any longer. I don't want to throw her away. I just want things to . . . like you said, evolve."

"How do you want the relationship to look know? What kind of friend do you want to be to her? What kind of friend is she able to be to you?"

"I never thought about the kind of friend I want to be to her," she says looking out the window while she considers the question. "I guess I want her to know that I'm always here if she needs someone to lean on. I'm just not interested in being her drinking buddy anymore."

"That's still a pretty good friend. What ways can she be of support to you?"

"Actually, she's probably already doing the things I need from her. She shows her support with logistics. I know she's not interested in the baby, or at least she looks really bored when I talk about him. But when I was in the hospital, she went out of her way to bring my favorite Thai food. She got this crazy nice gift for my shower, and last week she offered to pay for dinner since I was complaining that I'm worried about spending money while I'm on maternity leave. I guess she doesn't have to be interested in the baby, I'm just bummed that she seems bothered whenever I talk about him."

It is hard when the arrival of a baby changes friendships. In the postpartum year, we already feel underwater with the care and attention of the baby, attending to the other relationships in our lives can feel utterly overwhelming. The way in which Molly and Candace's friendship changed was completely normal. Molly's guilt and frustration with Candace was weighing heavily on her. Yet, even though Candace was acting out, she simultaneously demonstrated the ways she could still support and connect with her friend. We often resist or fear change, but change is necessary. Just as our relationship with our baby evolves over our lifetime, all our relationships need evolution.

Navigating your relationships with friends who are not parents or at least not yet parents can be challenging. When you feel like you are walking through a minefield, consider some of the following:

- **Talk about it with them.** If you feel your friend would be able to process with you, express some of your feelings and invite your friend to do the same. True connection comes from opening up and allowing yourself to be vulnerable, as well hearing out other people's experiences.

- **Forgive people's ignorance when possible.** Remember, you had no idea what you didn't know before you became a mother. I remember before I had kids, I complained of tiredness in front of a mom of teenagers who blurted out, "How can you be tired? You don't have kids!" To say I was annoyed would be a vast understatement. Now I get it. When we're tired parents, it can feel like we own the patent on fatigue.

- **If you don't feel they are capable of or in a place to process this with you, consider what type of relationship you want with this**

person. Again, don't just focus on what you want from the other person, but also what type of friend you want to be to them.

· **You may need to grieve the changes to the relationship or loss of your friendship as it was.** We forget to do this for reasons other than a death. Loss is loss. Grieve it if you're feeling a loss.

· **Just as you wish your friend would consider your perspective, pause a moment and remember what it is like for her.** Remember what it was like when your best girlfriend started dating someone. It felt threatening to see this person show up on the scene, waiting to see how their relationship changed yours. She is going through the same thing right now.

Pregnancy Loss or Infertility

"It's Lisa. I know she's been having trouble, but it really hurts that she can't be happy for me," Lauren says while we have lunch. Both our bellies are swollen with second trimester pregnancies.

"That must be really hard," I say, treading carefully. Lauren is one of my favorite people and her sister is not the easiest person to be around, but having struggled with infertility issues, I also connect with Lisa's experience.

I was extremely fortunate that the timing of my first pregnancy coincided with the pregnancies of several of my friends. However, each of them admitted trepidation to announce their news to me since they were well-apprised of my struggles to get pregnant over the course of two years. This included Lauren.

"I was so nervous to tell you that I was pregnant because I knew how much you struggled. Lisa hasn't been struggling nearly as long but she's acting like I got pregnant to hurt her feelings."

Lisa and Lauren have a close but contentious relationship in the way only twins can. Lisa was always labeled in the family as competitive, with "the killer instinct" consistent with her position as a litigation attorney. Lauren, a speech pathologist, is known as the family caretaker—including Lisa at times. I adore Lauren, but I understand Lisa's experience more than she realizes.

Infertility is the great equalizer. In many cases, it shows up unexpectedly. For those who have not dealt with it, it can be difficult to fathom the heartbreak of watching others get pregnant while you struggle with your own body's limitations or losses. This experience is not necessarily limited to those struggling to conceive. Over the years, I have seen many women in my practice who desperately wished to become mothers but circumstances (finances, lack of partnership, medical issues, lack of resources) prevented this dream of coming to fruition.

This disparity in experience can present a significant challenge to interpersonal relationships. New moms find that their friends who wished for children but are (yet) unable to have them sometimes become distant. This can feel like a mutual abandonment for both new mom and friend.

Ideas for managing relationships where "baby envy" presents:

- **Find a way to put this issue into words.** If you feel that you can process this in person, do so. Ask how they are feeling. Name your feelings of distance, guilt, or concern. If not, consider writing a letter or email.

- **Connect to empathy when possible.** Own your privilege in a thoughtful way.

- **Create space for yourself in the relationship.** Even women who struggle for years to have babies feel frustrated when the baby doesn't sleep. You are allowed to struggle, even with awareness of how fortunate you are to have a child.

- **Decide how you want to connect to your friend.** Does it feel best to leave the baby at home and spend time with your friend? Or are you able to remain connected with the baby around? If you can, check in with her as well.

- **Remember, there are no bad emotions here.** Envy, guilt, and resentment are still just emotions—not terminal conditions.

Mom-Mentors

Rachel and Joanna did everything before I did. They found their partners, got married, bought houses, found careers, and had babies before I did.

"How long was it before your kids slept through the night?" "What was it like when your water broke?" "What were your contractions like?" "How do you know what to do when a baby has croup?" "How long did you pump?" "How many times a day?" "How did you deal with engorgement?" "Sore nipples?" These are just a few of the many questions I have texted my two closest friends, often late at night.

Moms who had their kids before you had yours can be a godsend. Almost nothing can beat the reassuring voice of an experienced mom. They can seem unflappable compared to the steady hum of worry that sings in the ear of most new moms. When we are feeling new to motherhood and like an exposed nerve of vulnerability, a mom-mentor can feel like our own personal Yoda. These types of relationships can be reconnections of old friendships, a cousin, or existing friend who has children older than your baby.

The major challenge with mom-mentors (or any friend that has children older than yours) is that they are busy in different ways than you. If they have older children, your friend is probably out and about in activities with their older child. With differing and demanding schedules, carving out time to hang out can be challenging on the relationship. Therefore, mom-mentors may be relationships that connect primarily via text or email, or in a venue that happens to be mutually shared (e.g., a kid's activity class or workplace). That is okay. Respect it as a valuable connection all the same. Expect answers at quirky times—their lunch hour, late at night after their kids are in bed, or in a flurry of once per week when they are able to sit down and write a thoughtful response. Try not to personalize it if you don't hear from them as often as you'd like. It is not a reflection on your relationship, rather her busyness.

Milestone Mommies

In early motherhood, it can feel like no one understands your daily experience like those women with babies the same age as yours. I call these "milestone mommies," because we are around the same general developmental milestones as one another (both us and our babies). The endless fatigue of fragmented sleep, the mysterious fact that it can take two solid hours of work to get out the door for even the most casual event, the fact that your baby hates nursing under a coverup and you cannot be bothered to care any longer—no one gets it like someone walking a similar path.

These can be some of the easiest moms to meet. In early babyhood, there are many potential opportunities to attend groups to connect with someone who has a baby around the same age:

- Nursing support groups
- New moms' groups or groups for second-time (or more) moms
- Mom and baby yoga or movement classes
- Baby music or movement classes

These moms are potential long-term connections. Even though my oldest is in elementary school, nothing soothes my mommy worry more than hearing another mother report dealing with the same challenging experiences I encounter.

How to Connect

When I first met Kellie, her son and my daughter were preschoolers flipping over gymnastics bars while she and I madly tried to keep our younger children occupied for the forty-five-minute class. I liked her instantly. Her easy laugh and kind demeanor were a pleasure to be around. I appreciate my children's activities as a chance to interact with other parents. Sure, sometimes I am exhausted or on my phone trying to blast through emails like lots of other parents, but overall, whenever I make time to chat with some of the parents around me, I enjoy the connections. This can be an increasingly difficult exercise with our societal dependence on technology (namely our constant phone companions). This can be even more difficult when you already feel vulnerable in your postpartum year. Take the chance, though—it is important for our health.

In whatever way you choose, no matter what, find ways to connect. Mom-friends are some of the most important cornerstones in our villages. Now that we construct villages of choice, it is important to have an assortment of supports. Whether you use Peanut (informally known as the Tinder for mom-friends), or invite the woman in your breastfeeding group to lunch, the only thing that matters is to have some folks that get you. These connections are not a luxury, but a vital inoculation against the isolation of new mother-hood. In our conversation, Dr. Ziegler circled back to the UCLA study she cited on gender differences and stress. "When women are in the company of other women, oxytocin flows through our bodies in different ways than even if we're in the presence of a spouse or a male friend. Two women together get oxytocin flowing. How powerful is that? What a great argument for in-person connection! When I hear women say, 'but I'm really tired on Thursday night, I don't want to go for drinks,' I often say, 'I promise you, no one says they really regretted going for drinks that night with their dear friends. It doesn't happen. You feel energized, connected, and empathic.'"

Motherhood is a long and winding road. We need travel companions.

Notes

Ziegler, Sheryl. "Mommy Burnout with Dr. Sheryl Ziegler." Interview by Corinne Crossley, *Momma Bites! podcast,* February 26, 2019.

Ziegler, Sheryl. Ted Talk, Why Moms Are So Miserable, https://www.ted .com/talks/sheryl_ziegler_why_moms_are_miserable_dec_2017

Chapter 13:

Happy Momiversary!

"Happy Momiversary!" I comment on every Facebook birthday post of a kiddo in my feed. I say it as I hand over gifts at jumpy house birthday parties. I announce it as I hug my closest loved ones, even though their babies are teenagers. With the birth of a child, a mother is also born. As we near the end of the postpartum year, we experience mixed emotions with this milestone.

Freeedom!!!

When our babies round the bend on the twelve-month mark, we might feel relief. They have mastered sitting up, communication is getting easier, we can actually play with them. We have ways to take showers. We can get out the door in under forty-five minutes. We have learned how to deal with small emergencies like running out of diapers on the road, or medicating low fevers. Our babies are not totally reliant on our bodies (if we chose to nurse) for food.

Make no mistake, I am not saying life is easy now. In fact, some things are more challenging, with a determined baby. She crawls, cruises, toddles, or outright sprints. He grows impatient when signing for milk and we bring a lovey. When we want to get our hearts pumping with loops around the park, he whines, pointing to the swings.

Yet, as we start scouring Pinterest for original one-year-old birthday themes, we notice ourselves looking back. As with any milestone birthday, it is natural to reflect on where we were a year ago. This can bring up a variety of responses. It may feel bittersweet, empowering, triggering, or fill us with gratitude.

Grief

Some of us grieve the end of the postpartum year. For some moms, this is an extremely happy time, despite its challenges. The one-year mark can surface what moms know on a daily basis—our time with our babies is limited. We do not own them. They are their own people and will only continue to grow in that direction. Halfway through my daughter's first year, I was in a yoga class when a thought drifted into my head. *Parenthood is like holding a bird, teaching it to fly, and then letting go one feather at a time.* The thought was simultaneously comforting (one feather at a time gives me a lot more time with her) and devastating (letting go). I quietly sobbed through Savasana that day.

For some moms who dealt with a traumatic experience in the birth of their child or sometime this year, this retrospective can be triggering. If you have not yet sought therapy or support for your experience, please do not continue to delay in getting help. Please reach out to a postpartum specialist today. (Yes, still a postpartum specialist, even though you are at the end of the postpartum year.)

Exercise: Dear Momma

Write a letter to yourself on the morning before your child was born. Here are some points to consider:

- How you were feeling on that day—uncomfortable, scared, nervous, excited? Let that mom know how things went this year.
- What were the biggest challenges?
- What were the best things you never want to forget?
- What is your daily life like today?

Now, write a letter to yourself as a mom of an almost two-year-old. Here are some points to consider:

- What are your wishes for yourself?
- What will that version of you know that you want to know from her now?
- What are your hopes for her self-care?

_____

_____

_____

"___" Is the Best Age

"I once pitched a story to *Parents* magazine for an article called '_____ Is the Best Age.' I feel that every age that my kids have hit has been more challenging, but also really great. Every step of the way, it has gotten both more challenging and more satisfying."

—Lauren Smith Brody, author of *The Fifth Trimester* and founder of The Fifth Trimester movement

"Oh, look at that, it's nine o'clock. Do you know what I was doing seven years ago right now?"

"What?" my daughter asks, bursting with excitement for her birthday tomorrow, despite the late hour.

"I was sitting backward over the desk chair, breathing deep and concentrating while my body got ready for you to come out. When the pain, called contractions, would go away, I would walk in circles around our little house—living room, dining room, hall, kitchen, hall, dining room, living room."

"Hall, kitchen, hall," she finishes, enjoying the rhythm.

Every year, I tell my kids about the night they were born. I will continue to do so for as long as they will allow me, while I feel the pang of nostalgia with every passing year of our lives. Lauren Smith Brody's quote illustrates it perfectly. I still feel the visceral memories of those first days of skin-to-skin with my newborns. I still remember what it was like to nurse them. The downy touch of their baby hair against my cheek. My eyes tear just as I write these words. At the same time, I can tell them the story of their birth and hear their commentary about it. I find papers in my daughter's backpack with stories written by those same tiny hands that I saw on the ultrasound screen. In tickle fights, my son's kicks feel eerily similar to the same powerful in-utero thumps to my ribs. Babyhood can be a fabulous year and there are more wonderful things coming.

Continued Commitment to Self-Care

Self-care in the baby year can be incredibly difficult. Yoga with engorged breasts is torture. Going for a walk outside when we are on our fifth cold of the winter sounds terrible. Knowing our baby cried for forty straight minutes while we were reading a book at the library can undermine the most committed mom's resolve.

I applaud you for working so hard to connect to self-care. I promise this will serve you well in motherhood. As I wrote in the introduction, self-care does not make motherhood easy. Self-care makes it less hard. Offering ourselves some of the love and care we offer our loved ones is necessary nourishment in the work of motherhood. In taking care of ourselves, we demonstrate to our children how to take care of themselves.

> "You cannot serve from an empty vessel."
> —Eleanor Brownn, author

I know, you saw this quote in the introduction. Hopefully after reading this book you are even more connected to this idea and committed to keeping care for yourself in your life. The full quote is "Rest and self-care are so important. When you take time to replenish your spirit, it allows you to serve others from the overflow. You cannot serve from an empty vessel."

Be kind to your vessel.

Fill it often.

Notes

Smith Brody, Lauren. "Ending Maternity Leave? Talking 5th Trimester with Lauren Smith Brody." Interview by Corinne Crossley, *Momma Bites!* podcast, August 20, 2018.

Brownn, Eleanor. www.eleanorbrownn.com, last accessed January 16, 2019.

Resources

Chapter 1

- Cooling pads and pain comforts: https://fridababy.com/collections/mom

Chapter 2

- Find a doula on the DONA (Doulas of North America) international website: https://www.dona.org/what-is-a-doula/find-a-doula/
- Find a doula on the CAPPA (Childbirth and Postpartum Professional Association): https://cappa.net/directory/
- Find a lactation consultant: https://uslca.org/resources/find-an-ibclc
- To ascertain whether a provider is licensed, Google "check a professional license." Your state's database should be the first listing.
- Find an acupuncturist: Consult the "find a practitioner" function on the National Certification Commission for Acupuncture and Oriental Medicine: https://directory.nccaom.org/
- Find a chiropractor: search Palmer College of Chiropractic

Chapter 3

- *What No One Tells You: A Guide to Your Emotions from Pregnancy to Motherhood* by Alexandra Sacks and Catherine Birndorf. New York: Simon & Schuster Paperbacks, 2019.
- *Self-Compassion: The Proven Power of Being Kind to Yourself* by Kristen Neff, William Morrow Paperbacks, 2015.
- *Mommy Burnout: How to Reclaim Your Life and Raise Healthier Children in the Process* by Sheryl Ziegler, Dey Street Books, 2018.

Chapter 4

- La Leche site – www.llli.org
- D-MER: https://d-mer.org/
- http://www.ncsl.org/research/health/breastfeeding-state-laws.aspx

- La Leche League International. "Guide to Breastfeeding." Accessed November 15, 2019. https://www.llli.org/breastfeeding-info/
- *Work. Pump. Repeat.* by Jessica Shortall. New York: Abrams, 2015.
- *The Womanly Art of Breastfeeding* by Diane Wiessinger, Diane West, and Teresa Pitman. La Leche League. New York: Balantine, 2010.

Chapter 5

- *Intuitive Eating: A Revolutionary Program That Works* by Elyse Resch and Evelyn Tribole. New York: St. Martin's Griffin, 2012.

Chapter 6

- Morningist or eveningist questionnaire (MEQ) online: https://www.sleephealthfoundation.org.au/pdfs/World%20Sleep%20Day/Activity%20-%20Morning-Eveningness%20Questionnaire.pdf
- Society for Behavioral Sleep Medicine: https://www.behavioralsleep.org/
- American Academy of Sleep Medicine: https://aasm.org/

Chapter 7

- Postpartum Support International - https://www.postpartum.net/
- Postpartum Stress Center (for moms and providers) https://postpartumstress.com/
- *This Isn't What I Expected: Overcoming Postpartum Depression* by Karen Klieman and Valerie Raskin. Boston: Da Capo Press, 2013.
- https://www.americanprogress.org/issues/women/reports/2017/11/17/443051/suffering-in-silence/

For providers:

- The Every Mother Project - http://www.everymotherproject.org/
- The Perinatal Mental Health Alliance for People of Color - https://pmhapoc.org/

· Partners in perinatal health - http://www.piphma.org/

Chapter 8

- · Momma Strong: www.mommastrong.com
- · Curvy Yoga: www.curvyyoga.com
- · More to Love Yoga: www.moretoloveyoga.com
- · Mind-Body Barre: www.mindbodybarre.com

Chapter 9

- · *Health at Every Size: The Surprising Truth about Your Weight* Bacon, Linda. BenBella Books, 2010.
- · www.intuitiveeating.org – the official website of *Intuitive Eating* authors, Evelyn Tribole & Elyse Resch. Find Intuitive Eating trained professionals on this site.
- · www.marcird.com - Marci Evan's website, provides helpful resources on body image healing, including her newsletter.

Chapter 11

- · *Come As You Are: The Surprising New Science That Will Transform Your Sex Life* by Emily Nagoski. New York: Simon & Schuster Paperbacks, 2015.
- · *From Ouch! to Ahhh . . . The New Mom's Guide to Sex After Baby* by Sarah Swofford. Sarah J Swofford Media, 2014.

Chapter 13

- · *The Fifth Trimester: The Working Mom's Guide to Style, Sanity, & Success After Baby* by Lauren Smith Brody, Anchor, 2018.
- · *Work. Pump. Repeat.* by Jessica Shortall, Harry N. Abrams, 2015.
- · *Mommy Burnout: How to Reclaim Your Life and Raise Healthier Children in the Process* by Sheryl Ziegler, Dey Street Books, 2018.

Recipes

I love cooking and baking. I know this is not the case for everyone. If I could deliver you a steaming bowl of macaroni and cheese or some fresh baked cookies, I would. The second-best option is some of my recipes. The recipes that follow are low-pressure, mostly measuring cup-free, and should use a single pan plus a bowl, give or take. I hope these make your life manageable but delicious.

Greek Garden Omelet

Omelets are a godsend for a quick, balanced meal. Sometimes they can be a little tricky to slide out in one piece, so remember, any omelet that does not slide out of the pan can be delicious scrambled eggs. Rest assured, there's really no way to ruin this dish.

Ingredients

2 eggs
1 small pinch black pepper
1 pinch garlic powder
1 pinch onion powder
Handful fresh spinach
Palmful scallions
2–3 diced cherry tomatoes or 1 palmful diced tomatoes
1 palmful feta or Parmesan
2–3 olives, quartered, if that's your jam

Instructions

1. Crack eggs into a bowl and whisk. Season with pepper, as well as garlic and onion powders.
2. Heat skillet on medium heat until hot enough to sizzle a drop of water. If your skillet is nonstick, lubricate with a teaspoon or two of olive oil. If your skillet is not Teflon, spray well with cooking spray. If your spray burns immediately when you spray it, rinse out the skillet to cool it down, wait a second, then spray again. Dump eggs into pan and enjoy the fun sizzling sound.
3. Use the handle of the skillet to roll the eggs around to cook on the warmest edges of the pan. If you do not like any runny egg, and you live on the edge, flip the omelet using a spatula and immediately remove from heat.
4. When egg is set, top with all fixins either on one half or down the middle third of the omelet. If topping middle third, fold in two sides to close omelet. If you topped an entire side, just fold over the remaining side. Let stand for a few minutes so veggies can warm and cheese can get melty. For a heartier meal, make some toast, have some fruit or juice, and finish off with some tea.

5. Give yourself a hug for me. There's nothing cozier than an omelet. Every few weeks in my household, this is dinner, so don't hate on breakfast for dinner.

6. Other great omelet combinations include any kind of cheese, most any kind of vegetable (though some need to be pre-cooked, which can be a hassle), mushroom and bacon; pepper, onion, and cheese; or sausage and veggie.

Bacon & Egg Avocado Toast

Ingredients

Bread (sandwich/crusty/fancy—there is no right or wrong kind of bread)

½ avocado

1 slice pork, turkey, or veggie bacon (I prefer turkey, since I can make it in the microwave)

1 egg

Sriracha (optional)

Instructions

1. Toast the bread to your liking. If you like your toast barely crispy, you might want it a little darker for it to hold up.

2. Peel and slice avocado. Keep the pit in the other side and wrap tightly to prevent browning. Set aside for this same breakfast/snack/dinner tomorrow.

3. Mash avocado, and season to your liking. Spice options include salt, pepper, garlic powder, onion powder, cumin, paprika, chili powder, or dill.

4. Microwave your bacon. I microwave turkey bacon one minute per strip. I like mine really crispy.

5. Heat a small pan. If you want scrambled eggs, whisk your eggs. If you prefer over easy, just get your pan hot and well-oiled before cracking it in. Flip it as soon as the white is stable.

6. Spread mashed avocado on toast, top with crumbled bacon, eggs, and sriracha, if desired.

7. Like omelets, the options for avocado toast are endless. It can be a great way to use up ingredients. My sister's tip? Spread last night's guacamole on toast (pretty sure this is where the whole trend started).

M & C & B
(Macaroni & Cheese & Broccoli)

My kids ask for this weekly and it is just as easy as boxed mac and cheese, but a bit heartier.

Ingredients

1 (16 ounce) box of pasta, whatever shape you prefer (we are a rotini or penne household)

1 (12 ounce) bag frozen broccoli

1 package (2 cups) shredded cheese of your choice (Mexican is a favorite but cheddar, Colby-Jack, or sharp cheddar all work well too)

1 (12 ounce) can evaporated milk

Instructions

1. Boil pasta according to directions on box, subtracting three minutes from the cooking time. When your timer goes off, add ½ to ¾ bag of broccoli, depending on how much broccoli you want with your mac & cheese. Save the rest of the bag to supplement dinner next week.

2. Boil three additional minutes. It's fine if it is no longer at a rolling boiling with the broccoli in there. Then, drain pasta and return to pan. Empty cheese into pan on top of pasta. Pour in evaporated milk. Let sit for three minutes. Use this time to stare off into space, taking deep breaths.

3. Stir until cheese is incorporated. If you're hungry right now, eat this stove-top version. This is how my family loves this dish, especially with some sriracha stirred in. (The sauce is thinner.) If you want even more of that down-home feel, pour mixture into a greased 8 x 8 baking dish and bake at 350°F for 20 minutes or until bubbling.

Mama's Magic Oatmeal

My kids swear by my oatmeal and only my oatmeal. Here's my favorite way to do it.

Ingredients

½ cup (or whatever amount feels right to you) quick cooking oats
½ cup (or equivalent amount of oatmeal) 1% or higher milk
1 teaspoon cinnamon
½ banana, sliced
1 palmful favorite type of nuts

Instructions

1. Pour oatmeal, milk, and cinnamon into a bowl and give it a quick stir. Microwave for approximately 90 seconds. Stir. Top with bananas and nuts. Enjoy immediately.

New Mom Cookies
(Oatmeal Cherry Pecan Cookies)

These oatmeal cherry pecan cookies are one of my very favorites. They are a bit more of an effort, so if you're not feeling up to baking, hand over the recipe and ask someone else to make them for you. Like I said, when I nursed, I was convinced that oatmeal and nuts helped my milk production. Additionally, pelvic floor specialist Kathy Kates urges moms to eat plenty of fiber to prevent constipation. With these directives, I consider these cookies delicious medicine. Enjoy!

Ingredients

1 cup flour
½ teaspoon salt
1 teaspoon cinnamon
¼ teaspoon baking soda
¼ teaspoon baking powder
½ cup (1 stick) butter, softened
⅔ cup dark brown sugar
⅓ cup granulated sugar
1 egg
1 teaspoon vanilla extract
1½ cup old fashioned oats
¾ cup dried cherries or any type of dried fruit (raisins, diced apricots, etc.)
⅓ cup chopped pecans (or any type of nut, chopped)

Instructions

1. Preheat oven to 350°F. Combine flour, salt, cinnamon, baking soda, and baking powder in a bowl and set aside.
2. In a separate bowl, beat butter and sugars together until fluffy. Add egg and vanilla to butter mixture and beat until incorporated. Add flour mixture, beating to form a batter. Add oats, cherries, and nuts, beating only to distribute ingredients evenly.
3. Line cookie sheets with parchment or a silicone mat for easy removal and to prevent the cookies from burning. Drop dough in tablespoon-sized balls, leaving two inches between cookies. Bake for 12 to 14 minutes. Or, if you prefer freshly baked cookies every day, place portioned cookie dough in the freezer on a cookie sheet. Chill for twenty minutes and then place in a Ziplock bag. Whenever you want freshly baked cookies, remove a few from the freezer and leave them on a greased cookie sheet to soften while the oven preheats. Bake and enjoy fresh cookies as often as you like.

Acknowledgments

A mom is only as strong as her village, and this book is a direct reflection of mine: My mom and dad, as well as my in-laws Bob and Monica whose unwavering support always keep my head above water. My sister, who continues to set examples for me, well past childhood. Peter, Derek, Becky, Annika, Sarah, Julia, Emma, and Parker, I'm honored to call you my family.

For my village of choice—my golden girls, Rachel and Joanna, I'd never have survived early motherhood without you. To Jessica and Megan, two of the smartest clinicians and coolest ladies I've had the pleasure to know. Special love to my original *Momma Bites!* cohost Jess who pushed me out of the nest and said "you got this." Thank you to my readers, Ally, Amy, and Kelly. I know only too well the commitment it takes for a mom to find time and energy to stay awake to read anything other than *Goodnight Moon*. For all the mom-friends who asked in gymnastics lessons, at pre-school signup, hair appointments, and at birthday parties, "How's the book coming?" Your kindness felt like a welcome cheer to a tired marathoner. Behind any great provider are other great providers—special thanks to my supervisor Amber. And to Heidi, who started this whole thing when she taught me about self care, and then years later reminded me, people don't want to hear from someone who does things perfectly, they want to hear from humans. I am so very human.

A special thanks to Linda Shanti McCabe, whose words inspired the strength and spark to make this book happen when I didn't think it could. To my village of experts—Kathy Kates, Emily Silver, Suzanne Riendau, Joy Rober, Angela Hawthorne, Divya Kumar, Andrea Wuotila, Dianne Cassidy, Elyse Resch, Courtney Wyckoff, Toni Liechty, Sarah Coyne, Margie Davenport, Anna Guest-Jelley, Patrice Carroll, Sarah Swofford, Marci Evans, Sheryl Ziegler, and Lauren Smith Brody—truly, this book does not happen without you. Lindsay Stenovec, the work you're doing for moms soothes my heart. (Watch out world, her book is next!)

Special love to my clients, who inspire me every day. It is a deep honor to know you and be a member of your self-care army.

To all the mommas out there—awake in the middle of the night, dragging through the day, beaming with love, or sobbing with fear, I see you.

Index

A

acceptance, 51–52

acupuncture, 35–39
  and babies, 38–39
  finding an acupuncturist, 36
  needles, 35
  postpartum conditions treated by, 36
  questions for acupuncturist, 36–37
  reasons for, 38
  sessions, 37–38

Acupuncture & Oriental Medicine society, 36

affirmations, good enough, 55–56

Affordable Care Act, 84

African-American women, 127–128

Ahhh...The New Mom's Guide to Sex After Baby (Swofford), 194

alone time, x

American College of Obstetricians and Gynecologists, 19

American Journal of Public Health, 128

American Physical Therapy Association, 31
  Certificate of Achievement in Pelvic Physical Therapy (CAPP), 31
  Women's Health Clinical Specialist (WCS) certification, 31

anger, 120, 123

Aniston, Jennifer, 189

anxiety, ix, 49–50, 121, 127, 198. *See also* Postpartum mood and anxiety disorders (PMADs)

appetite, lack of, 120–121

avoidance, 50–51, 123

B

baby
  and acupuncture, 38–39
  ambivalence about, 12
  behavior, 27
  blues, 13–15, 118–119
  brain, 107
  care, assistance, 17, 27
  care, right way, 56
  classes, 220
  colic, 39
  co-sleeping, 115
  digestive issues, 39
  food, making your own, 48–49
  food allergy signs, 75
  lack of interest in, 120
  love for, 11–12
  rashes, 39
  thoughts of harming, 121
  urge to hurt, 7
  verbal cues, 108
  weight gain, 28–29
  worry about, 196

baby nurse, 26–27
  finding, 27–28
  services, 27

Bacon, Linda, 159

The Badass Breastfeeder (Cassidy), 28, 62, 81

Becker, Carolyn Black, 101

bed, getting out of, 120

biofeedback, 141

bipolar disorder, 123

Birndorf, Catherine, 18, 54

birth, 2–4
  caesearan section, 3–6, 127
  expectation *vs.* reality, 2–3
  injuries, 32, 36
  premature conditions, 39
  spacing, 108
  traumatic, 4, 31, 127

birthday, baby's, 224–228

bladder, 5

bleeding. *See also* Blod clots; Lochia
  and exercise, 147
  postpartum, 6
  severe, 7

blood clots, 4–7

body image, 152–180, 196, 208–209, 211
  body parts purpose, 165–167
  "body positive," 162
  body talkers, 161
  clothing, 170–172
  comparison, 175–176
  dietitian, 178–179
  diets, 161
  eating disorder, 161
  factors contributing to, 160–161
  family messages, 160
  fitness industry, 161
  friend messages, 160
  gyms, 167
  improvement, 161–165
  influencers, 161
  media consumption, 160–161
  meditation, 176–177
  past weight gain/loss, 161
  pitfalls, planning for, 172–175
  professional help, 178–179
  and sex, 200–201
  sports and body-based activities, 161
  support, 177–178
  therapy, 178–179
  using your body, 168–169

body shaming, 148

books or magazines, 10

Boston NAPS, x, 4, 54

bottle feeding, 9. *See also* Formula

boundaries in relationships, 209